CALAMITY AT
CHANCELLORSVILLE

The Wounding and Death of
Confederate General Stonewall Jackson

Mathew W. Lively

SB

Savas Beatie
California

Library of Congress Cataloging-in-Publication Data

Lively, Mathew W.
Calamity at Chancellorsville : the wounding and death of Confederate General Stonewall Jackson / Mathew W. Lively.
pages cm
Includes bibliographical references and index.
ISBN 978-1-61121-138-2
1. Jackson, Stonewall, 1824-1863—Death and burial. 2. Generals—Confederate States of America—Biography. 3. Confederate States of America. Army—Officers—Biography. 4. United States—History—Civil War, 1861-1865—Biography. 5. Chancellorsville, Battle of, Chancellorsville, Va., 1863. I. Title.
E467.1.J15L58 2013
355.0092—dc23
[B]
2013006687

Published by
Savas Beatie LLC
989 Governor Drive, Suite 102
El Dorado Hills, CA 95762

Phone: 916-941-6896
(E-mail) customerservice@savasbeatie.com

05 04 03 02 01 5 4 3 2 1
First edition, first printing

Savas Beatie titles are available at special discounts for bulk purchases in the United States by corporations, institutions, and other organizations. For more details, please contact Special Sales, P.O. Box 4527, El Dorado Hills, CA 95762, or you may e-mail us at sales@savasbeatie.com, or visit our website at www.savasbeatie.com for additional information.

Proudly published, printed, and warehoused in the United States of America.

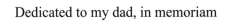
Dedicated to my dad, in memoriam

Table of Contents

Table of Contents, continued

Dramatis Personae

THOMAS JONATHAN JACKSON
National Archives

Born in Clarksburg, Virginia (now West Virginia) on January 21, 1824. Graduated from the United States Military Academy at West Point, New York in 1846 and served with distinction during the Mexican-American War. Served as an instructor at the Virginia Military Institute in Lexington, Virginia, prior to the start of the Civil War. At 39, Jackson was a lieutenant general and commander of the Second Corps of the Army of Northern Virginia in the Confederate army.

MARY ANNA MORRISON JACKSON
and JULIA LAURA JACKSON
Virginia Military Institute Archives

Born in Charlotte, North Carolina on July 21, 1831. Mary met Thomas J. Jackson while visiting her sister in Lexington, Virginia and married him on July 16, 1857, at the Morrison home in North Carolina. She was 31 years old when she visited Jackson prior to the start of the battle of Chancellorsville.

Julia was born in Charlotte, North Carolina on November 23, 1862, and named after Jackson's mother (Julia) and his sister (Laura). She was the third and only surviving child of Thomas J. Jackson and was five months old when she accompanied her mother on her visit prior to the battle of Chancellorsville.

**DR. HUNTER HOLMES
McGUIRE**
Author's Collection

Born in Winchester, Virginia on October 11, 1835. Graduated from Winchester Medical College in 1855 and originally enlisted in the Confederate army as a private. He was promoted instead to brigade surgeon under Thomas J. Jackson and then to major and medical director of the Second Corps when Jackson assumed command of the unit. Only 27 years old at the time of the battle of Chancellorsville, he was already a well-respected surgeon in the army.

JAMES POWER SMITH
Author's Collection

Born in New Athens, Ohio on July 4, 1837. Graduated from Union Theological Seminary in Hampton Sydney, Virginia, in 1861 and enlisted in the artillery service for the Confederate army later that year. He was appointed to the position of aide-de-camp to Jackson in 1862 and was 25 years old during the battle of Chancellorsville.

**ALEXANDER SWIFT
PENDLETON**
Author's Collection

Born in Alexandria, Virginia on September 28, 1840. Graduated from Washington College in Lexington, Virginia in 1857 and left graduate school at the University of Virginia to enlist in the Confederate army in 1861. He was 22 years old and served on Jackson's staff as assistant adjutant general of the Second Corps during the battle of Chancellorsville.

JOSEPH GRAHAM MORRISON
Author's Collection

Born in Lincoln County, North Carolina on June 1, 1842. He was the brother of Mary Anna Jackson and was a cadet at the Virginia Military Institute in Lexington, Virginia, when the Civil War started. He left the Institute in 1862 to enlist in the Confederate army and serve as a volunteer aide-de-camp on Jackson's staff. He was 20 years old at the time of the battle of Chancellorsville.

JEDEDIAH HOTCHKISS
Author's Collection

Born in Windsor, New York on November 30, 1828. Graduated from the Windsor Academy and worked as a schoolteacher and mining geologist prior to the start of the Civil War. He offered his services to the Confederate army as a mapmaker and became the chief topographical engineer for the Second Corps in 1862. He was 34 years old at the time of the battle of Chancellorsville.

BEVERLY TUCKER LACY
Author's Collection

Born in Prince Edward County, Virginia on February 19, 1819. Graduated from Washington College in Lexington, Virginia in 1843, and studied at Princeton Theological Seminary in Princeton, New Jersey. In March 1863, at the age of 44, he was appointed by Jackson to be the unofficial chaplain to the Second Corps.

ROBERT EDWARD LEE
Library of Congress

Born in Westmoreland County, Virginia on January 19, 1807. Graduated second in his class from the United States Military Academy at West Point, New York in 1829. Lee was a career army officer and served with distinction in the Mexican-American War. He refused overall command of the Union army in 1861, and instead resigned his commission when Virginia seceded from the Union. At age 56, he held the rank of general in the Confederate army and was commander of the Army of Northern Virginia.

JAMES EWELL BROWN STUART
Library of Congress

Born in Patrick County, Virginia on February 6, 1833. Graduated from the United States Military Academy at West Point, New York in 1854. He resigned his commission and joined the Confederate army in 1861. He was 30 years old at the time of the battle of Chancellorsville and was a major general in command of the cavalry of Lee's Army of Northern Virginia.

AMBROSE POWELL HILL, JR.
Library of Congress

Born in Culpeper County, Virginia on November 9, 1825. Graduated from the United States Military Academy at West Point, New York in 1847. Briefly served in the Mexican-American War and joined the Confederate army in 1861. He was a major general at 37 years old and commanded the "Light Division" in Jackson's Second Corps.

JOSEPH HOOKER
Library of Congress

Born in Hadley, Massachusetts on November 13, 1814. Graduated from the United States Military Academy at West Point, New York in 1837. Served in the Mexican-American War and resigned from the army in 1853. He re-enlisted at the start of the Civil War and rose to the rank of major general. He was in command of the Union Army of the Potomac during the battle of Chancellorsville.

Introduction

Civil War history abounds with stories and anecdotes regarding Stonewall Jackson. Next to Robert E. Lee, no individual became more revered in the South and beloved by its people. Admiration for his personal nature and military prowess transcended national borders and extended not only into the North but also across the ocean to Europe. An editorial by John W. Forney appearing in the *Daily Morning Chronicle* (Washington D.C.) three days after Jackson's death expressed the views of many in the North when he wrote: "While we are only too glad to be rid, in any way, of so terrible a foe, our sense of relief is not unmingled with emotions of sorrow and sympathy at the death of so brave a man." Forney went on to observe that Jackson was not the first instance of "a good man devoting himself to a bad cause." After reading the editorial, Abraham Lincoln sat down and wrote a personal note to Forney: "I wish to lose no time in thanking you for the excellent and manly article in the *Chronicle* on 'Stonewall Jackson.'"[1]

One hundred and fifty years later, Jackson's life continues to fascinate people. Orphaned as a young boy, steely determination carried him from the rural mountains of what is now West Virginia to graduation from the United States Military Academy. His accomplishments on the battlefield and untimely death at the height of his greatest military victory then propelled him to legendary status. "He fell at the summit of glory," one subordinate wrote, "before the sun of the Confederacy had set, ere defeat, and suffering and selfishness could turn their fangs upon him."[2]

Despite the abundance of praise and adulation, Thomas Jonathan Jackson the man remains somewhat of an enigma. His character and lifestyle were full of contrasting elements: ambition with humility, constancy with eccentricity, simplicity with a complex sense of duty, and gentleness with ruthlessness in battle. Perhaps the best description of Jackson's persona is

---

1 *Daily Morning Chronicle* (Washington D.C.), May 13, 1863, in Abraham Lincoln, *Collected Works of Abraham Lincoln*, ed. Roy P. Basler, 9 vols. (New Brunswick, NJ, 1953), vol. 6, 214.

2 Richard Taylor, *Destruction and Reconstruction: Personal Experiences of the Late War* (New York, NY, 1879), 80.

that offered by biographer Douglas Southall Freeman: "He lives by the New Testament and fights by the Old."[3]

A tendency toward modesty and secrecy in both his personal and professional lives has left minimal direct sources from which to draw a picture of his personality. He did not live to write his memoirs, few personal letters survive, and he did not grant interviews during the war. What we know of Jackson's life comes primarily from the postwar writings of family members, friends, and fellow soldiers.

The complexities involved in telling the story of Jackson's life persist in telling the story of his death. First-person accounts of his wounding at the battle of Chancellorsville and subsequent passing eight days later survive, but they are replete with contradictions and omissions—even, at times, within separate accounts written by the same individual. Some descriptions were written within days of the event, while others came 20, 30 or even 50 years later, when facts tend to blur and merge with the romantic memories of days gone by. As a result, several controversies surrounding his wounding and death continue to be debated to this day.

This account of Jackson's last 20 days is based on the author's interpretation of the evidence compiled from multiple primary sources. The story is told in a narrative style to make it more pleasing to read, but not at the cost of historical accuracy. Quotations and conversations are transcribed exactly as recorded in the primary source from which they were taken. A more scholarly examination of the interpretations in the narrative is contained in an appendix for those interested in the historical debate. A second appendix discusses the rapid evolution of Jackson's image during and after the Civil War.

Although the extent of the effect can be debated, Stonewall Jackson's death undoubtedly influenced the course of the Civil War; both amateur and professional historians enjoy playing out such "What if?" scenarios. The legacy of his military career and the oddity of his character have appealed to people from all walks of life for 150 years. As one of Jackson's former cadets noted, "He is not Virginia's alone: God gave him to the world."[4]

---

3   Douglas S. Freeman, *Lee's Lieutenants*, 3 vols. (New York, NY, 1942), vol. 1, xlii.

4   James E. Goode, *The Life of Thomas J. Jackson by a Cadet* (Richmond, VA, 1864), 196.

Acknowledgments

Writing a well-researched book is a daunting task and one not performed without the assistance of others. It is not possible to thank everyone who contributed to the completion of this work and I apologize to those not specifically mentioned who, nonetheless, played a part in its development.

My thanks to the numerous librarians, archivists, and curators of the depositories that provided the primary source material and photographs used throughout the book, most notably: the Library of Congress, the Virginia Historical Society, the Library of Virginia, the Museum of the Confederacy, the Virginia Military Institute, and the West Virginia University Regional History Collection.

A special thanks to the staff of the Fredericksburg and Spotsylvania National Military Park, of which the Chancellorsville battlefield and the Stonewall Jackson Shrine are part. The unlimited access they provided me to their vast source of primary material was invaluable to the completion of the book. In particular, I would like to thank Frank O'Reilly, park historian, who long ago encouraged me to undertake this project and put it on paper. I am indebted to him for unselfishly providing me with his knowledge and guidance over the years.

To all my friends and colleagues who reviewed the manuscript or parts of it, providing me with their much appreciated advice and critique. Each one knows the individual part he or she played in the final product. Thanks also to Hal Jespersen for the excellent, high-quality maps he produced for the book.

Finally, I want to thank all the individuals associated with Savas Beatie, LLC, especially those with whom I worked directly: Rob Ayer, Lindy Gervin, Veronica Kane, and Sarah Keeney. Your professionalism and assistance throughout the publishing process were outstanding. Most of all, I would like to extend a special thanks to Ted Savas for accepting the manuscript for publication. Without his support, none of this would be printed.

Mathew W. Lively
Morgantown, WV

Prologue

The American Civil War raged across the nation's landscape from 1861–1865, a short 78 years after the United States had won its independence from England. While an exact toll of the resulting casualties is unknown, an estimated 620,000–750,000 Americans died as a direct result of the conflict. Although sociopolitical differences between the states north and south of the Mason-Dixon Line had existed since the birth of the nation, the presidential election of 1860 served as the catalyst for the bloodiest war in American history.[5]

Stewing in anger over Abraham Lincoln's election to the presidency on a platform vowing to prohibit the expansion of slavery into territories that had yet to become states, seven states in the Deep South (Alabama, Florida, Georgia, Louisiana, Mississippi, South Carolina, and Texas) seceded from the Union in 1861 and formed the Confederate States of America. Hostilities between the two governments began in April of the same year when Confederate forces fired upon the federal garrison at Fort Sumter, South Carolina. The eventual surrender of the fort compelled Lincoln to call for 75,000 volunteer troops to "suppress" the actions of the seceded states and "to cause the laws to be duly executed." Lincoln's action triggered the four remaining southern states (Arkansas, North Carolina, Tennessee, and Virginia) to quickly leave the United States and also join the Confederacy, setting the stage for civil war.[6]

The first major clash between the two woefully inexperienced armies occurred on July 21, 1861, near the Manassas railroad junction in central Virginia, 25 miles southwest of Washington, D.C. Known as the battle of

---

5 Drew G. Faust, "Numbers on Top of Numbers: Counting the Civil War Dead," in *Journal of Military History* (October 2006), issue 4, 997. Historians for decades have accepted the oft-cited death toll of 620,000 as the best estimate of Civil War mortality, a calculation Faust maintains is "a product of extensive post-war reconstruction—a combination of retrospective investigation and speculation that yielded totals that posterity has embraced as iconic." More recent and extensive research places the actual number of deaths closer to 750,000. See J. David Hacker, "A Census-based Count of Civil War Dead," in *Civil War History* (December 2011), issue 4, 307-348.

6 Abraham Lincoln Papers, April 15, 1861, Series 1, General Correspondence, Library of Congress.

First Manassas by the South (which often named battles after the nearest town) and First Bull Run by the North (which often named battles after the nearest body of water), the contest ended with an unexpected Confederate victory, as Union forces hastily retreated to Washington.

Fighting in the eastern theater of the war did not resume in earnest until the spring of 1862, when the newly organized Federal army moved by water from Washington, D.C., to the peninsula between the York and James rivers outside the Confederate capital of Richmond, Virginia. Advancing to the outskirts of the city, the Union army was within seven miles of ending the Civil War barely one year after the start of the conflict.

Meanwhile, in the Shenandoah Valley of northwestern Virginia, a relatively unknown Confederate general by the name of Thomas J. Jackson was completing one of the most brilliant tactical campaigns in military history. Over a period of 30 days, Jackson's outnumbered force marched 350 miles and defeated 3 separate Union armies in 5 distinct battles. His maneuvers prevented the Union army from sending 40,000 soldiers to the peninsula as reinforcements, while his own army eventually slipped away to Richmond to help defend the capital.

Once Jackson's army arrived in Richmond, a series of engagements known as the Seven Days' battles began on June 25, 1862. The fighting culminated on July 1 with an overall Confederate victory, as the Union army was driven from the Richmond vicinity. In addition to saving the city from capture, the sequence of battles also yielded one of the South's most significant events of the war: the emergence of Gen. Robert E. Lee as commander of the Confederate army.

With the Federals safely removed from Richmond, the Confederate army moved north toward Washington, where it met another Union force near the previous battleground around Manassas junction. The battle of Second Manassas on August 29–30, 1862, was another decisive southern victory, emboldening Lee to carry the war into northern territory.

In early September, the Rebel army crossed the Potomac River into Maryland and advanced into the western half of the state beyond the city of Frederick. The battle of Antietam was triggered when the pursuing Union army caught up with the Confederates near Sharpsburg, Maryland, on September 17, 1862. After a 12-hour fight that produced 23,000 casualties, the single bloodiest day in American history ended with a Confederate withdrawal to Virginia. This long-awaited Union victory in the east prompted Lincoln to issue the Emancipation Proclamation five days later on September 22, 1862. The proclamation only freed the slaves of the Confederate states, and left those in states loyal to the Union in bondage.

However, the act did effectively transform the Civil War into an epic struggle to end slavery.

The warring armies moved south following Antietam, meeting again on December 13, 1862, in the city of Fredericksburg, Virginia. After repeated Federal assaults against a strongly fortified Confederate position failed, the battle ended in yet another defeat for the Union army. With the subsequent arrival of cold weather, the two armies ceased fighting and went into winter quarters.

Chapter One

A Little Gem

The winter of 1862–1863 passed with the two greatest armies of the Civil War camped within sight of each other across the Rappahannock River around the city of Fredericksburg, Virginia. Occupying the city on the south side of the river were 60,000 men in the Army of Northern Virginia from the Confederate States of America under the command of Gen. Robert E. Lee. The opposite river bank was held by soldiers belonging to the Army of the Potomac from the United States of America, 130,000 strong and under the new command of Maj. Gen. Joseph "Fighting Joe" Hooker.

A revolving door of Union generals in the previous 18 months had produced three prior leaders of the Army of the Potomac; with Hooker obtaining command after his superior, Maj. Gen. Ambrose E. Burnside, was soundly defeated by Lee's Confederates at the battle of Fredericksburg in December 1862. Hooker, an aggressive and often boastful general who actually disliked his "Fighting Joe" nickname, was nonetheless confident in his ability to succeed where his predecessors had failed. As winter turned to spring and Hooker prepared his men for a new offensive, he bragged of having "the finest army on the planet," and announced, "may God have mercy on General Lee, for I will have none."[1]

Five miles south of Fredericksburg near the station of Hamilton's Crossing on the Richmond, Fredericksburg & Potomac Railroad, Lt. Gen. Thomas J. Jackson anxiously awaited the arrival of his family. Jackson, the 39-year-old commander of Lee's Second Corps, stood nearly six feet tall, with an angular body attached to unusually large feet. He had a sharp nose and brown hair with a full beard that took on a more rusty color in sunlight. Most strikingly, he had piercing, deep-blue eyes that one staff officer described as looking "straight at you and through you almost as he talked." Those close to Jackson often remarked how the color of his eyes seemed to intensify with the passion of battle. He was an intensely religious individual whom author Douglas Southall Freeman portrayed as being "of contrasts so complete that he appears one day a Presbyterian deacon who delights in theological discussion and, the next, a reincarnated Joshua." Not one to waste words, Jackson tended to speak in short, terse sentences that were always to the point, and his customary affirmative response was a simple, "very good."[2]

Jackson bordered on hypochondria. He suffered from various medical ailments, both real and imagined, the treatment of which rendered the impression of a somewhat eccentric personality. As a teenager, he had been diagnosed as having dyspepsia, a condition that caused him to suffer from intermittent stomach pains throughout his life. To control the symptoms, Jackson often followed a strict diet of simple foods that focused on cornbread, butter, and milk. Years of service in the artillery had affected his hearing and he was nearly deaf in one ear. He tried to read only during the day, as poor light caused him to complain of eye strain. When sitting, he maintained a rigid posture with a ramrod-straight spine so his internal organs would stay in their proper alignment. He also had the strange belief that one

---

1   John Bigelow, *Chancellorsville* (New York, NY, 1995), 108; Stephen W. Sears, *Chancellorsville* (Boston, MA, 1996), 120.

2   Hunter H. McGuire, "Reminiscences of the Famous Leader by Dr. Hunter McGuire, Chief Surgeon of the Second Corps of the Army of Northern Virginia," in *Southern Historical Society Papers (SHSP)* (1891), vol. 19, 304; Freeman, *Lee's Lieutenants*, vol. 1, xlii; James Power Smith, *Stonewall Jackson and Chancellorsville. A Paper Read Before the Military Historical Society of Massachusetts, on the First of March, 1904* (Richmond, VA, 1904), 7.

arm was heavier than the other, which he periodically corrected by raising the extremity into the air to allow the blood to flow back into the body, so as to lighten it. Prior to the Civil War, Jackson served as an instructor at the Virginia Military Institute in Lexington, and his oddities of character prompted some cadets at the school to call him "Tom Fool."[3]

But now in the spring of 1863, as the war entered its third year of brutal fighting, he was known throughout both the North and South as "Stonewall" Jackson. He had earned the nickname two years earlier as a brigadier general at the first battle of Manassas (or Bull Run, as it was called in the North) when he and his brigade stood their ground against a Union counterattack while other Confederate units retreated. Called "Old Jack" by the soldiers of his army, Jackson had developed a reputation—in contrast to his "Stonewall" nickname—for the ability to rapidly move his forces over long distances. "He was more like a thunderbolt of war than a stonewall," remarked Maj. Gen. Jubal A. Early, one of Jackson's divisional commanders.[4]

The warm spring weather signaled that renewed fighting was imminent and Jackson had been eagerly expecting his wife's brief visit before the start of the campaign. Mary Anna Morrison—known to her family and friends as Anna—had married Jackson in 1857 while he was an instructor at VMI. Described as "fair in person and beautiful in character," Anna had dark hair with matching eyes and was seven years younger than Jackson. It was his second marriage, his first wife having died after the birth of a stillborn son in 1854.[5]

3 Clement D. Fishburne, Special Collections, University of Virginia (UVA); Dabney H. Maury, *Recollections of a Virginian in the Mexican, Indian, and Civil Wars* (New York, NY, 1894), 71. Thomas Jonathan Jackson was born in Clarksburg, (West) Virginia, on January 21, 1824, and was raised by his uncle Cummins Jackson near Weston, (West) Virginia. In 1846, Jackson graduated from the United States Military Academy at West Point and served with distinction in the Mexican War. He resigned his commission in 1852 to become Professor of Natural and Experimental Philosophy and Artillery Tactics at the Virginia Military Institute (VMI) in Lexington, Virginia. Jackson remained at VMI until the outbreak of the Civil War, when he received a commission as colonel in the Virginia volunteers in April 1861.

4 William McLaughlin, *Ceremonies Connected with the Unveiling of the Bronze Statue of Gen. Thomas J. (Stonewall) Jackson at Lexington, Virginia, July 21, 1891* (Baltimore, MD, 1891), 35.

5 James I. Robertson, *Stonewall Jackson: The Man, The Soldier, The Legend* (New York, NY, 1997), 175. Jackson and Anna Morrison married on July 16, 1857. His first wife had

Belvoir Mansion. Home of the Thomas Yerby Family.
Fredericksburg and Spotsylvania National Military Park

On April 20, 1863, Anna arrived at Guiney Station, a railroad stop ten miles south of Hamilton's Crossing, after traveling from her father's home in North Carolina where she had been living since the start of the war. Accompanying Anna was the Jacksons' five-month-old daughter, Julia, whom her father was about to meet for the first time. She was the couple's second but only surviving child, their first daughter died of jaundice 25 days after being born in 1858.[6]

Jackson was patiently waiting at the station as the train carrying his family pulled in at noon under a steady spring rain. Julia had just awakened from a nap, and she "never looked more bright and charming," according to Anna. As Jackson entered the coach and eagerly walked back to greet his

---

been Elinor Junkin, whom he married on August 4, 1853. Elinor, or "Ellie," as she was called, died of a hemorrhage following childbirth on October 22, 1854.

6 Their first child, Mary Graham, was born on April 30, 1858. Julia Laura was born on November 23, 1862.

family, the first sight of his child caused a broad smile to spread across the features of the otherwise serious-minded general. "His face was all sunshine and gladness," Anna recalled. "It was a picture, indeed, to see his look of perfect delight and admiration as his eyes fell upon that baby." Catching "his eager look of supreme interest in her," the infant "beamed her brightest and sweetest smile upon him in return, so it seemed to be a mutual fascination." The proud father wanted desperately to hold the smiling infant, but the oilcloth overcoat he wore was still dripping wet, so he refused to take the baby in his arms. Not until they arrived at the house and he had tossed the coat aside did he hold his daughter for the first time.[7]

At Hamilton's Crossing, Jackson had arranged for his family to stay at Belvoir, the Georgian-style home of plantation owner Thomas Yerby. The stately brick mansion rested on a hill only a mile from the tent Jackson had established as his corps headquarters. Despite the presence of his wife and daughter, the duty-bound Jackson "did not permit the presence of his family to interfere in any way with his military duties," Anna wrote. "The greater part of each day he spent at his headquarters, but returned as early as he could get off from his labors, and devoted all of his leisure time to his visitors."[8]

At Belvoir, the proud father was enthralled with his blue-eyed infant daughter, seldom letting her out of his sight. Carrying her in his arms, he would occasionally stop at a mirror so he could hold her up and say, "Now, Miss Jackson, look at yourself," or he would show her to members of the Yerby family and ask, "Isn't she a little gem?" When the child was asleep, he was often found kneeling over her cradle, silently staring at her small, angelic face. To the frequent remark that she resembled him, he would always reply, "No, she is too pretty to look like me." The child's presence caused such a stir among the men, who were eager to see "little Miss Stonewall," that Jackson allowed them to be marched on parade past the house while Julia was held in a spot where the troops could see her.[9]

On Thursday, April 23, Julia was baptized in the parlor of the Belvoir mansion while another spring rain steadily poured outside. The ceremony

7   Mary Anna Jackson, *Life and Letters of General Thomas J. Jackson* (New York, NY, 1892), 423.

8   Ibid., 426.

9   Ibid., 423; Henry Kyd Douglas, *I Rode with Stonewall* (Chapel Hill, NC, 1940), 217-218.

was performed by the Reverend Beverly Tucker Lacy, or Tucker Lacy as he was known, a Presbyterian minister and friend of Jackson who had recently started service as the unofficial chaplain of the Second Corps. Described by a fellow minister as "a genial gentleman, an indefatigable worker, and a powerful and effective preacher," Lacy's association with Jackson "gave him special influence and a wide range of usefulness."

Originally planned as a small, private ceremony among just the Jacksons and Yerbys, the baptism quickly became a much larger affair after Jackson allowed several of his staff members to attend the service at their request. One of those present fondly recalled how the start of the ceremony was delayed for some unexplained reason, prompting the impatient Jackson to leave the room in a "decided way" and return moments later with the child in his arms, ready to be baptized.[10]

The weather was pleasant the following Sunday morning when Anna attended a church service with her husband. Reverend Lacy preached "a solemn and powerful sermon" on the parable of the rich man and Lazarus to a crowd of over 1,500 soldiers, including General Lee and several staff officers. Anna was impressed by Lee's appearance, remarking "how handsome he looked, with his splendid figure and faultless military attire." After the service, Jackson spent the remainder of the afternoon with his wife discussing spiritual matters. "He seemed to be giving utterance to those religious meditations in which he so much delighted," she recalled.[11]

These days at Belvoir with his wife and only child nearby were happy times for Jackson, and Anna had never seen him in better health. At her request, he agreed to sit for a photograph while wearing a "handsome" new military dress coat given to him by his friend and colleague, Maj. Gen. James Ewell Brown "Jeb" Stuart, the dashing cavalry officer of the Army of Northern Virginia. Stuart had commissioned one of Richmond's best tailors to make Jackson a gray coat out of fine wool, complete with brass buttons, gold arm bands, and white cuffs and collar. Uncomfortable wearing such ornate attire, Jackson had rarely donned the coat in public. Reflective of his Spartan nature, he had recently cut the gold braid off a new cap Anna had sent him so he could tie it in the hair of an admiring five-year-old girl, telling

10 J. William Jones, *Christ in Camp or Religion in Lee's Army* (Richmond, VA, 1887), 96; Jackson, *Life and Letters*, 424-425.

11 Jones, *Christ in Camp*, 488; Jackson, *Life and Letters*, 425.

Last photograph of Stonewall Jackson.
National Archives

her, "It suits a little girl like you better than it does an old soldier like me." He then wrote to his wife, saying he was ashamed of wearing a hat with gilt braid, reminding her that "I like simplicity."[12]

After arranging his hair, which Anna said was "unusually long for him, and curled in large ringlets," Jackson posed for the three-quarter-length photograph while sitting in a chair placed in the hallway of the Yerby house. While the picture was being taken, a stiff breeze blew through an open door and into Jackson's face, causing him to frown slightly. The resulting photograph portrayed him with a stern expression that Anna felt did not reflect his natural appearance. His soldiers disagreed, believing it an accurate representation of Old Jack, and the image would become a favorite among the men. Taken less than two weeks before his death, it would be Stonewall Jackson's last picture.[13]

In the dawn hours of April 29, while the couple still slept, an officer arrived at the Yerby house with an urgent message for the general. "That sounds as though something stirring were a foot," Jackson said to Anna as he quickly dressed and headed downstairs. Major General Jubal A. Early had sent an adjutant to notify the general that Hooker's army was crossing the Rappahannock. The messenger reported that elements of the Union army were using the cover of a heavy morning fog to advance across the river at Franklin's Crossing, two miles south of Fredericksburg.[14]

Returning upstairs, Jackson reluctantly informed Anna that he must leave immediately for the front. He sensed the start of a major battle, so, out of concern for the safety of his family, he advised her to take the baby and leave for Richmond by train. After what Anna described as a "tender and hasty good-bye" to her and Julia, he put on the new dress coat she preferred and left the Yerby house without eating breakfast.[15]

---

12 Ibid., 422; Douglas, *I Rode With Stonewall*, 214; Roberta C. Kinsolving, "Memories of Moss Neck in the Winter of 1862-63," *Confederate Veteran (CV)* (January 1912), 26. The girl was Janie Corbin, who lived at the house in Moss Neck where Jackson had spent the winter prior to moving to Hamilton's Crossing. Jackson became quite attached to the little girl, but shortly after he moved to Hamilton's Crossing, Janie died of scarlet fever. When told of the child's fate, Douglas wrote that Jackson "was much moved and wept freely."

13 Jackson, *Life and Letters*, 427.

14 Anna Jackson, "Last Days," in Dabney-Jackson Collection, box 2, Library of Virginia (LVA).

15 Jackson, *Life and Letters*, 430.

Jackson rode from Belvoir to an area of high ground south of Fredericksburg overlooking the Rappahannock River. Sitting erect on his horse as artillery shells burst around him and bullets from enemy pickets whistled past his head, Jackson calmly took out a pair of binoculars and surveyed the Federal movement below. His men on the bluff watched the spectacle nervously, expecting at any moment to see their beloved general take a bullet and fall to the ground. It was not unusual, however, for Old Jack to expose himself to such danger. Earlier in the war when asked by a subordinate officer how he remained so calm when under fire, Jackson replied: "My religious belief teaches me to feel as safe in battle as in bed. God has fixed the time for my death. I do not concern myself about that, but to be always ready, no matter when it may overtake me."[16]

Finished with his observations, Jackson leisurely placed his field glasses in their case and rode back to the main line. William J. Seymour of the 1st Louisiana brigade remarked how the men were surprised to see Jackson no longer wearing the "old rusty, sunburnt gray coat and faded blue cap" they were accustomed to seeing, but instead his "unusually spruce appearance" in the new coat "excited much attention and remark" among his admiring soldiers.[17]

Although Jackson would have preferred to return to Belvoir and personally see his family off to Richmond, the start of battle did not afford him the luxury of time. He scribbled a quick note to his wife and handed it to Lt. Joseph G. Morrison, brother of Anna Jackson and aide-de-camp on his staff. He instructed Morrison to return to the Yerby house and escort Anna and Julia back to Guiney Station, where he wanted them to board the morning train. Morrison, however, wished to remain close to the action and suggested that Tucker Lacy go instead. Sending the chaplain was better, Morrison argued, since Jackson would most likely need his staff around during the battle. Jackson agreed and handed the note to Lacy, who quickly left for Belvoir.

Back at the Yerby house, Anna had just finished packing when Reverend Lacy arrived in an ambulance wagon to carry the family to the

16 John D. Imboden, "Incidents of First Bull Run," *Battles and Leaders of the Civil War (B&L)*, 4 vols. (New York, NY, 1884-1887), vol. 1, pt. 1, 238.

17 William J. Seymour, *The Civil War Memoirs of Captain William J. Seymour. Reminiscences of a Louisiana Tiger*, ed. Terry L. Jones (Baton Rouge, LA, 1991), 49.

train station. She read her husband's note explaining why he could not be there to say good-bye and telling her that he had asked for God's blessing upon them in their speedy journey.

Anna's visit had lasted a mere nine days, but it was filled with loving memories of spending time with her husband and watching him dote on their infant daughter. Now, with cannon booming in the distance and wounded soldiers beginning to arrive at the Yerby house, Anna headed south—unaware that the next time she would see her husband, he too would be a casualty of the battle she was leaving behind.

Chapter Two

We Will Attack Them

Neither a town nor a village, Chancellorsville was a sizable two-and-a-half story brick house, along with several outbuildings, which sat at the intersection of Ely's Ford Road and the Orange Turnpike. In 1813, a group of investors had developed a 36-mile toll road from Orange Court House, Virginia, east to Fredericksburg. Three years later, in order to accommodate travelers on the new turnpike, George Chancellor built a large tavern ten miles west of Fredericksburg and ambitiously named the area Chancellorsville. At the height of its status, the tavern contained a post office and was considered by many to be "one of the most celebrated houses in Virginia." Upon George Chancellor's death in 1836, his widow turned operation of the inn over to other family members until her own death in 1860, after which the family shut the tavern down to travelers. When the battle started in 1863, Frances Chancellor, daughter of the widow Chancellor, was living in the house with her own son and six daughters.[1]

---

1 Noel G. Harrison, *Chancellorsville Battlefield Sites* (Lynchburg, VA, 1990), 16. For a more detailed history of the house and the Chancellor family, see Ralph Happel, "The

Photograph of an intersection along the Orange Plank Road.
Wood planks buried in the roadway are visible in the foreground.
Library of Congress

Wagoners had found the original 1813 turnpike surface difficult to traverse due to its thick red clay that became almost glue-like when wet. Subsequent attempts to improve road conditions by adding a macadamized, or crushed stone, surface were largely unsuccessful. In the 1850s, another group of investors sought to improve the route by building an all-weather lane consisting of wooden planks buried just beneath the road surface. This newly constructed path, renamed the Orange Plank Road (or the Plank Road, as it was more often called), followed the original turnpike right-of-way

Chancellors of Chancellorsville," in *The Virginia Magazine of History and Biography* (1963), vol. 71, issue 3, 259-277.

except in two places where it diverged in order to take advantage of easier grades. The new and old roads ran as one for six miles west out of Fredericksburg until the Plank Road looped slightly south, paralleling the original path, which became known as the Old Turnpike. Converging again at Chancellorsville, the roads again ran as one for another two miles before splitting a second time at Wilderness Church, a white-painted Baptist structure sitting in a clearing 150 yards north of the divide. The roads then remained separate for the remaining distance from Wilderness Church to Orange Court House. For several miles on each side of Chancellorsville, the Plank Road and the Old Turnpike traveled through a 70-square-mile area of dense trees and thick, tangled underbrush known as the Wilderness of Spotsylvania or, more simply, the Wilderness.

Four miles north of Chancellorsville, the easterly flowing Rapidan River empties into the Rappahannock, which then continues on a bending, 14-mile course southeast to Fredericksburg. During the Civil War, two primary crossings over the Rappahannock existed at Banks' Ford, five miles west of Fredericksburg, and United States (U.S.) Ford, located a short distance north of the Chancellor house. Northwest of Chancellorsville, the Rapidan River had crossings at Ely's Ford and six miles farther to the west at Germanna Ford. The Orange Plank Road, the Old Turnpike, and the roads from Ely's and U.S. Fords all converged at Chancellorsville, making the location a critical access point into Fredericksburg from the west.

*   *   *

General Joe Hooker had developed a sound plan to defeat the Confederates, one that would meet with initial success. He intended to move the bulk of his forces to Chancellorsville and thus into the rear of Lee's army while simultaneously threatening a direct assault west out of Fredericksburg. If successful, the Confederates would be trapped in a vise, with a retreat south as their only means of escape.

The first step in Hooker's plan was to send Maj. Gen. George Stoneman's cavalry force south to disrupt Lee's communication and supply lines along the Richmond, Fredericksburg & Potomac Railroad. Two weeks later on April 27, Hooker put the rest of his plan in motion by sending three Union corps on a long flanking march across the Rappahannock 30 miles north of Fredericksburg. Once across the river, the force split in two and headed south toward Chancellorsville. Half of the army then crossed the

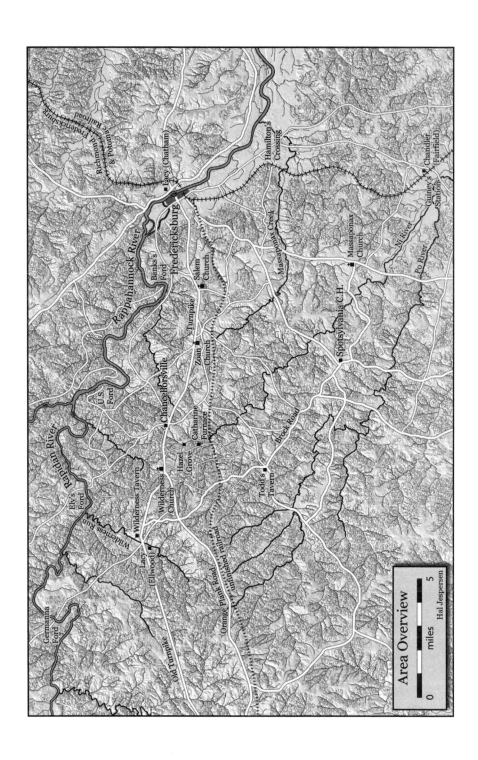

Area Overview

Hal Jespersen

0   miles   5

Rapidan at Germanna Ford while the other half crossed at Ely's Ford. It took the Confederates two days to detect the Union movement, and by the time they discovered it on April 29, nearly 40,000 enemy soldiers were successfully across the Rappahannock.

To create a diversion from the flanking movement taking place to the north, Hooker sent two Union divisions across pontoon bridges below Fredericksburg at Franklin's Crossing and Fitzhugh's Crossing. Hoping to trick Lee into believing the main attack was occurring at this point, Union forces crossed the river on the foggy morning of April 29—the day Jackson had been aroused from sleep—and began engaging the Confederates around Fredericksburg. The following day, Hooker sent another Union corps across the Rappahannock at U.S. Ford to join the main army that was now assembling at Chancellorsville.

Over a period of several days, Hooker managed to place four Union corps, roughly 70,000 men, in Lee's rear at Chancellorsville, while leaving another two corps at Fredericksburg to threaten the Confederate front. At that point, Joe Hooker was pleased with himself and his army. He had placed the Rebels in a vise, and all he needed to do was close it. True to character, on April 30, he imprudently sent General Order No. 47 to the Army of the Potomac, stating, "[T]he operations of the last three days have determined that our enemy must either ingloriously fly, or come out from behind his defenses and give battle on our own ground, where certain destruction awaits him."[2]

Since taking command in the summer of 1862, Robert E. Lee had transformed the Army of Northern Virginia into an effective and confident military force that other Union generals had learned the hard way not to underestimate. A West Point graduate and career army officer, the 56-year-old Lee seemed to possess the uncanny ability to read the minds of his opponents. When Ambrose Burnside was appointed as the new commander of the Army of the Potomac prior to the battle of Fredericksburg in December 1862, Lee dryly commented to Lt. Gen. James Longstreet, "I

---

2 Joseph Hooker to Army of the Potomac, April 30, 1863, in *The War of the Rebellion: A Compilation of the Official Records of the Union and Confederate Armies*, 128 vols. (Washington, D.C., 1880-1901), Series 1, vol. 25, pt. 1, 171. Hereafter cited as *OR*. All references are to Series 1 unless otherwise noted.

fear they may continue to make these changes till they find someone whom I don't understand."[3]

Although Lee was never tricked into believing the advance below Fredericksburg was the primary assault, he had uncharacteristically allowed Hooker to seize the advantage by amassing a force of superior size behind his position. He now had a choice to make: withdraw quietly, or fight it out—on one or, quite possibly, two fronts. It was an easy decision for Lee in the end, as it was not in his nature to "ingloriously fly" from the field and leave without a fight. He decided to accept Hooker's challenge and give the bombastic general a chance to live up to his "Fighting Joe" nickname. Lee's response would involve an aggressive battle plan that fully employed the military talents of Stonewall Jackson, his trusted lieutenant.

*   *   *

Early on Thursday morning, April 30, Jackson was making arrangements for breaking camp in preparation of the upcoming battle. "Hold my horse," he instructed his servant, Jim Lewis, as he entered his headquarters tent and closed the flap. Lewis was a slave whom Jackson had hired from William Lewis of Lexington at the start of the war to work as his camp orderly. Described by one of Jackson's staff as "brave and big-hearted," Lewis was a beloved figure among the general's inner circle, and was one of the few individuals Jackson allowed to openly question his wishes. On one occasion during the battle of Fredericksburg, Jackson had instructed the servant to saddle his favorite horse, "Little Sorrel." Jim had protested, saying the animal had been ridden in battle the previous day and needed rest. "An amusing war of words passed between them," Anna Jackson wrote, "but Jim had it in his power to gain the victory, and brought out another horse, which the general mounted, and rode off."[4]

---

3   James Longstreet, "The Battle of Fredericksburg," in *B&L*, vol. 3, pt. 1, 70.

4   Hunter H. McGuire and George L. Christian, *The Confederate Cause and Conduct in the War Between The States* (Richmond, VA, 1907), 210; Jackson, *Life and Letters*, 385. Little is known about the background of James Lewis, or Alexander, as some references cite his last name. Jackson reportedly hired Lewis for the war at $12.50 per month. After Jackson's death, Lewis worked as camp servant for Lt. Col. Alexander S. Pendleton, formerly of Jackson's staff, until Pendleton's death at the battle of Fisher's Hill in

By this time in the war, Little Sorrel was almost as distinctive in the Confederate army as Jackson. Originally purchased in 1861 as a present for Anna, Jackson had found the horse's gait so smooth that he declared, "A seat on him was like being rocked in a cradle." Described by one staffer as a "natural pacer with little action and no style," Little Sorrel did not fit the mold of the prototypical "war-horse." Small in stature at only 15 hands tall, (five feet at the shoulder) the horse was noted for its calmness and remarkable endurance on long marches. Soldiers were often surprised to watch the horse "lie down like a dog" and rest when Jackson dismounted during pauses in a march.[5]

A commotion of camp activity broke out after Jackson had entered his tent, prompting Lewis to raise his hand and call out, "Hush. The general is at prayer." An immediate silence descended over the area. Fifteen minutes later, a confident Jackson emerged from the tent, jumped on his horse, and set off to find Lee.[6]

The weather was cool, with a slight drizzle falling, and General Lee, who was suffering from what his physicians termed rheumatism, was conducting business from inside his tent near Fredericksburg. Before long, Jackson arrived and went inside to report on the enemy's movement below the city. The two generals soon emerged from the tent, mounted their horses, and rode back to the ridge overlooking the Rappahannock to better survey the situation below Fredericksburg.

Peering through the haze, Lee and Jackson observed the enemy's crossing and the formidable Union artillery placements on the opposite river bank. Recognizing that most of the Federal army had been removed from this line for the advance on Chancellorsville, Jackson wanted to attack the Union forces here, as the Confederates now had an advantage in numbers. Lee thought otherwise. Pointing to the strong artillery positions across the river, he said, "It would be hard to get at the enemy and harder to get away if

---

September 1864. Lewis subsequently died during the winter of 1864. See *Atlanta Daily Constitution*, May 3, 1878.

5 "Stonewall Jackson's War Horse," *New York Times*, November 27, 1887; Douglas, *I Rode with Stonewall*, 206-207. Jackson paid the Confederate government $150 for the Morgan horse after his army captured a livestock train at Harper's Ferry, (West) Virginia, in April 1861. Originally named "Fancy," the horse quickly become known as "Little Sorrel" once Jackson started using the gelding as his regular mount.

6 Beverly Tucker Lacy, "Narrative," in Dabney-Jackson Collection, box 2, LVA.

we drove him into the river." Ever confident in Jackson's abilities, however, Lee added, "But, General, if you think it can be done, I will give orders for it." Jackson paused a moment before answering. He considered Lee a "phenomenon," and had once remarked how the distinguished southern commander was "the only man whom I would follow blindfold." If Lee was questioning the success of an attack, the situation undoubtedly deserved more consideration. Jackson asked the commanding general if he could have more time to examine the ground before making a decision. Lee agreed and turned back toward headquarters while Jackson rode off into the mist for further reconnaissance.[7]

The morning fog lifted around noon, offering Jackson a clear view of the enemy's position. His opinion aligned with that of Lee as he examined the area from several angles, so he resigned himself to the reality that a strike against the Federal forces would have to occur on different ground. Anticipating that ground would be around Chancellorsville, Jackson wanted quick and detailed information of the area. He immediately sent for his resourceful and talented mapmaker, Jedediah Hotchkiss.

Hotchkiss was a Virginia geologist and school teacher who, despite never receiving an actual commission in the Confederate army, had been serving as the topographical engineer on Jackson's staff for over a year. Hotchkiss was working in his tent when he received a message that the general wanted to see him. Arriving at the front, he was instructed by Jackson to "strike off eight maps" of the region west of Fredericksburg between the Rapidan and Rappahannock rivers and another one extending 35 miles west to the town of Stevensburg, Virginia.[8]

Jackson then returned to Lee's headquarters with his assessment of a strike below Fredericksburg: "It would be inexpedient to attack there," Jackson acknowledged. Lee in the meantime had devised another plan. Contrary to military principles, he intended to split his smaller army in the face of the larger enemy. His risky plan called for 10,000 men to guard what effectively would become the Confederate rear at Fredericksburg while he

7   Fitzhugh Lee, "Chancellorsville – Address of General Fitzhugh Lee before the Virginia Division, A. N. V. Association, October 29th, 1879," in *SHSP* (1879), vol. 7, 562; John Esten Cooke, *Stonewall Jackson: A Military Biography* (New York, NY, 1866), 212.

8   Jedediah Hotchkiss, *Make Me a Map of the Valley: The Civil War Journal of Stonewall Jackson's Topographer*, ed. Archie P. McDonald (Dallas, TX, 1973), 136.

swung the bulk of his army west to confront Hooker's massive force at Chancellorsville. Lee instructed Jackson to leave one division at Fredericksburg and move his remaining corps at dawn to the Orange Plank Road, where he was to "make arrangements to repulse the enemy."[9]

*   *   *

Stonewall Jackson was the embodiment of a warrior. A stickler for military discipline and regulations, he believed "the business of the soldier is to fight." In March of 1861, as the furor over secession and possible war raged among cadets at the Virginia Military Institute, Jackson addressed a group of fiery students with the words, "The time for war has not yet come, but it will come, and that soon; and when it does come, my advice is to draw the sword and throw away the scabbard." Those who knew Jackson often spoke of how his steely-blue eyes would "flash" with excitement at the time of battle, and the various health issues that seemed to plague him during periods of inactivity were curiously absent when fighting was near. Having received Lee's instructions to move out the next morning, a "smiling and elated" Jackson was in high spirits on the evening of April 30 as he anticipated the upcoming battle.[10]

In camp that night at Hamilton's Crossing, Tucker Lacy commented that there was talk of the Confederates withdrawing. "Who said that?" Jackson shot back. "No sir, we have not thought of retreat, we will attack them." He then asked Lacy to come inside his tent so the two could speak privately.[11]

Prior to serving as chaplain for the Second Corps, Lacy had been pastor of the Fredericksburg Presbyterian Church and had knowledge of the area's geography—information Jackson desperately needed. He asked Lacy whether he knew the roads leading to Chancellorsville, and listened intently while the pastor described three routes.

---

9   Fitzhugh Lee, "Chancellorsville," 562; *OR* 25, pt. 2, 762.

10   G. F. R. Henderson, *Stonewall Jackson and the American Civil War*, 2nd ed. (London, England, 1913), vol. 2, 481; Jennings C. Wise, *The Military History of the Virginia Military Institute from 1839 to 1865* (Lynchburg, VA, 1915), 133; Lacy, "Narrative."

11   Ibid.

"Could you guide a column there in daylight," Jackson asked, "or could you get me guides?"[12]

Lacy thought one of the Yerby boys would serve as the best guide. Agreeing with the pastor, Jackson welcomed the opportunity to pay a visit to the family, as he had not seen them in several days and was unsure when he would have another chance. By the time Jackson and Lacy arrived at Belvoir, however, the Yerbys were already in bed. Out of respect for the family, Jackson refused to have them awakened, and instead headed back to camp.

Three nights shy of full, the moon softly illuminated the road as Jackson and Lacy walked back to camp. As the two talked, Jackson expressed concern that Union forces would attack the small Rebel force guarding the roads between Fredericksburg and Chancellorsville near a structure called Zoan Church. Sitting on high ground seven miles west of Fredericksburg, the area around the church was currently occupied by forces under the command of Confederate Maj. Gen. Richard H. Anderson. The position was vital to Lee's strategy, and if Hooker occupied the ridge before Jackson could reinforce Anderson the next day, the entire Confederate battle plan would be in jeopardy.

"Why not march up tonight?" Lacy asked, "The moon is bright."[13]

Jackson thought for a moment. He generally did not like to march troops at night, but, looking around the moonlit landscape, he began to consider the option. Once Lacy assured him that more guides could be found to lead the troops at night, Jackson decided to commence the movement early. He sent Lacy off to recruit the guides while he began to notify his division commanders to prepare to move before dawn.

---

12 Ibid.

13 Ibid.

Chapter Three

Press On

Stonewall Jackson arrived at General Anderson's position stretching across the Plank Road and the Old Turnpike west of Fredericksburg at 8:30 a.m. on May 1, 1863. The rainy and cool weather of the previous few days had given way to more pleasant conditions—"a genuine May day," as cartographer Hotchkiss recorded in his journal. Jackson arrived at Zoan Church well ahead of his three divisions that were rapidly marching along the roads from Hamilton's Crossing.

In compliance with previous orders, Anderson's men were actively digging and building breastworks to prepare for a defensive stand against the Union force occupying Chancellorsville. Jackson immediately ordered the soldiers to drop their shovels and prepare to advance on the enemy. Although Lee's instructions were to "make arrangements to repulse the enemy," the aggressive Jackson decided the best way to repulse the Federals was to attack them. The order to advance came as no surprise to artillery colonel Edward P. Alexander, who, when he saw Jackson coming up the road, knew immediately that "all our care and preparation at that point was work thrown away."[1]

It was several hours before enough of Jackson's men had arrived to begin an advance; meanwhile, Hotchkiss had also arrived and distributed his newly drawn maps to the division commanders. Finally, at 10:30 a.m., Jackson gave the order to move out. He sent two columns marching toward Chancellorsville, one along the Old Turnpike and the other on the lower Plank Road.

Three miles to the west, General Hooker was ordering an advance out of Chancellorsville along the same two roads. Anticipating little resistance, he intended to have his troops directly in the rear of Fredericksburg by evening. Unaware that Anderson had been reinforced, Hooker thought his army would encounter only a small force of Confederates dug in at Zoan Church; instead, as his men marched into clearings outside of Chancellorsville, they walked headlong into the advancing Rebel army.

The initial contact between the two forces occurred on the Old Turnpike as Confederate skirmishers from a Virginia regiment met a unit of Federal cavalry from Pennsylvania. The fighting prompted Maj. Gen. George Sykes, commander of the Union forces marching along the turnpike, to order his lead brigade ahead at the double-quick. Driving the Rebel skirmishers back, Sykes' men encountered the advancing Confederate army under Maj. Gen. Lafayette McLaws, at which point "quite a brisk little engagement" ensued.[2]

Meanwhile, along the Plank Road to the south, the lead elements of the Union army under Maj. Gen. Henry W. Slocum were advancing more cautiously. Moving rapidly toward them from the other end of the road was Richard Anderson's division, followed by the men of Jackson's corps. The combination of Sykes' double-quick movement on the upper road and Slocum's tentative advance on the lower path caused an unequal distribution of Union forces across the parallel roads. Slocum's location on the Plank Road when he met Anderson's men was nearly two miles behind Sykes' position on the Turnpike to the north.

1 Hotchkiss, *Make Me a Map of the Valley*, 137; Fitzhugh Lee, "Chancellorsville," 562; Edward P. Alexander, *Fighting for the Confederacy: The Personal Recollections of General Edward Porter Alexander*, ed. Gary W. Gallagher (Chapel Hill, NC, 1989), 196.

2 *OR* 25, pt. 1, 862.

Jackson quickly realized that his forces were in an ideal position to unleash his favorite surprise attack: the flanking maneuver. Recognizing that his men on the lower Plank Road were in line with the Union forces on the Turnpike above, Jackson turned Brig. Gen. Robert E. Rodes' division north, directly into the right flank of the upper Federal army.

George Sykes' position suddenly became perilous. He was extended and isolated from the rest of the Union forces, hotly engaged in his front, and now the enemy was closing in on his flank. He needed help soon, and he sent a message to Hooker informing him of the critical situation.

* * *

Back at headquarters in the Chancellor house, Hooker was realizing that his grand strategy to defeat Lee was no longer going as planned. He had underestimated the boldness of the Southern commanders, just as others had before him. It had been easier during his time as a subordinate general, because there was always someone else to blame for apparent inaction. But now, as commander of all Union forces, "Fighting Joe" himself balked. When Hooker learned of Sykes' dilemma, he decided to order all forces back to Chancellorsville rather than provide the reinforcements Sykes had requested. Months later, when asked about the battle, he was said to remark, "For once I lost confidence in Hooker, and that is all there is to it."[3]

As the Union army withdrew to the safety of its Chancellorsville defenses, Stonewall Jackson's men were hot on their heels. "Always mystify, mislead, and surprise the enemy," Jackson once advised, "and when you strike and overcome him, never let up in the pursuit so long as your men have strength to follow." Jackson also received a dispatch from Gen. Jeb Stuart that his cavalry force to the west was closing in on Chancellorsville from the south. "I trust that God will grant us a great victory," Jackson wrote back to Stuart. "Keep closed on Chancellorsville."[4]

Running due west out of Fredericksburg and two miles south of Chancellorsville was the path of an unfinished railroad. The route ran east-west a short distance below the Plank Road and had been graded but not

---

3 Bigelow, *Chancellorsville*, 478.

4 John D. Imboden, "Stonewall Jackson in the Shenandoah," in *B&L*, vol. 2, pt. 1, 297; "Field Notes at Chancellorsville from Stuart and Jackson," in *SHSP* (1883), vol. 11, 138.

yet laid with rails, making it a good road for infantry. In a continued effort to outflank the Union army by moving left, Jackson sent a brigade of Georgians west on the right-of-way to link up with Stuart's cavalry.

The two groups of Confederates met in the Wilderness a mile and a half southwest of Chancellorsville at a structure called Catharine Furnace. Built in 1837, the furnace was part of an iron ore industry that had developed in the Fredericksburg area in colonial times, and the near-impenetrable woods of the region were a testament to the extent of its past operations. The old-growth timber of the area had long ago been harvested on a massive scale to provide charcoal for the furnace. In its place grew the dense entanglement of brambles, second-growth pine, and scrub oak that gave the Wilderness its name. The furnace had stopped production in the 1840s, due in part to a lack of available timber, but was reactivated in 1862 to supply iron for the Confederacy. Charles C. Wellford, who lived nearby with his family, was the proprietor and operator of the furnace.

Robert E. Lee arrived on horseback as Jackson was pushing his men along the Plank Road and directing McLaws to "press on up the turnpike toward Chancellorsville." After a brief consultation, Lee rode north to reconnoiter other potential avenues for advance against Hooker, while Jackson and his brother-in-law, Joseph Morrison, headed southwest into the Wilderness.[5]

Riding down the Furnace Road, Jackson and Morrison met Jeb Stuart at Catharine Furnace. Pleased to find each other in the dense woods, the two generals briefly discussed the situation before deciding to take a better look at the Union position. To their left, a Confederate battery had posted itself on a small knoll, and the group rode to the top for a better view. Jackson and Stuart were unable to see the right of the Union position from the crest of the hill, but they did observe Yankee cannon less than a mile away on a patch of high ground at a farm called Hazel Grove. With the Georgia infantry positioned on the unfinished rail bed below, Jackson ordered the men to advance through the woods toward the Union forces. As the Confederate battery opened fire in support of the movement, Union cannon from Hazel Grove and beyond barraged the knoll with a murderous return volley. As exploding shells began kicking up dirt around them, Stuart remarked,

5   *OR* 25, pt. 1, 764.

"General Jackson, we must move from here." Moments later, a shell fragment struck Stuart's adjutant, mortally wounding him.[6]

With evening falling and the advance at Catharine Furnace checked by the strong Union position on Hazel Grove, Jackson left the woods and rode back to the Old Turnpike to assess progress on that front. To his dismay, he discovered that Federal resistance was stiffening everywhere, as Hooker's forces had withdrawn back into the defenses they had left at the start of the day. It was nearly 7:30 p.m., and a frustrated Jackson now made his way back to the intersection of the Plank and Furnace Roads, where he again met General Lee. A Yankee sharpshooter perched in a distant tree was shooting at nearby artillerymen, so the generals dismounted and took shelter in a line of trees along the side of the road. Sitting down on a log, Lee motioned for Jackson to sit next to him. The two leaders reviewed the day's action and began to form a battle plan for the next day—a plan that would eventually become even more daring than the last. After the war, while touring the battlefield during an interview, Joe Hooker would point to the spot where Lee and Jackson sat and lament it as being the place where "the mischief was devised which came near ruining my army."[7]

*   *   *

As the sun set on the first day of the battle of Chancellorsville, Robert E. Lee and Stonewall Jackson sat together on the fallen log in the thick forest of the Wilderness. So far, their gamble had paid off: the Rebel army's sudden attack had surprised Hooker and caused him to withdraw his forces back into a defensive position. Now Lee and Jackson needed to devise a plan that would keep the pressure on Chancellorsville while trusting the two Union corps at Fredericksburg to remain stationary and not overrun the solitary division the Confederates had left behind.

Jackson thought the Yankees were on the run and would keep running. They had yet to attack Fredericksburg and, when pressed, their army had

6 Joseph G. Morrison, "Stonewall Jackson at Chancellorsville," in *CV* (May 1905), 231; Marcellus N. Moorman, "Narrative of Events and Observations Connected with the Wounding of General T. J. (Stonewall) Jackson," in *SHSP* (1902), vol. 30, 110.

7 Bigelow, *Chancellorsville*, 262; T. M. R. Talcott, "General Lee's Strategy at the Battle of Chancellorsville," in *SHSP* (1906), vol. 34, 17; Samuel P. Bates, "Hooker's Comments on Chancellorsville," in *B& L*, vol. 3, pt. 1, 218.

quickly retreated to Chancellorsville. "By tomorrow morning there will not be any of them on this side of the river," Jackson exclaimed. Lee saw it differently. While he hoped Jackson was correct in his projection, he was of the opinion that Hooker was going to stay where he was and wait for the Confederates to attack. If Lee was correct and the Federals were still in front of them in the morning, he wanted to be ready with a plan to resume the battle. He opened a map and began studying the layout.[8]

The two started their discussion by describing what each had discovered in reconnaissance that afternoon. Lee had ridden to the right of the Old Turnpike and found no room on that side to get around the Union army. Jackson related how the attack on the other end at Catharine Furnace had stalled due to the strong Federal position on the high ground at Hazel Grove. That left the middle of Hooker's line. It was likely to be well-defended, but perhaps it could be broken by a direct assault.

They needed more information on Hooker's strength to be sure. Nightfall was quickly approaching, but the nearly full moon would provide sufficient light for a reconnaissance of the Union defenses. The generals summoned Lee's aide, Maj. Thomas M. Talcott, and Jackson's chief engineer, Capt. James Keith Boswell, a young Virginian whose nickname was "Preserves" because he was so fond of eating jelly. They sent Talcott and Boswell to scout the Federal line and ascertain whether a frontal assault was possible.

As Lee and Jackson continued to discuss the possibilities of where and how to attack Hooker, Jeb Stuart arrived with news that would abruptly change the focus of their conversation. Stuart reported that Fitzhugh Lee, nephew to the commanding general and one of Stuart's brigade commanders, had ridden unmolested to the extreme right of the Federal position and discovered that Hooker's right flank, three miles west on the Plank Road, was "in the air," or unsecured by any natural obstacle. Additionally, the Union defensive breastworks on that end of the line faced south, not west. Lee and Jackson realized their golden opportunity: if the Rebel army could march far enough to the left, it could outflank the Union position and attack the unprotected end of that line.

The keys to completing such a maneuver would be secrecy, speed, and good roads. They needed roads of sufficient size to move a large body of

---

8 Lee, "Chancellorsville," 567.

infantry and artillery through the Wilderness while remaining out of the Federals' view. Stuart was not sure whether such roads existed, but he offered to find out. With a wave of his plumed hat, the cavalier officer jumped back on his horse and galloped off into the darkness.

Talcott and Boswell returned to the roadside headquarters around 10:00 p.m. and reported that a frontal assault was out of the question. Hooker had set up a strong defensive arc across the front of Chancellorsville, which, in combination with the thick woods, left little opening for attack. That settled the matter in the mind of the commanding general: they would go after Hooker's right flank.

"How can we get at these people?" Lee asked, as he stared at the map by candlelight.

"You know best," Jackson replied. "Show me what to do, and we will try to do it."[9]

Later in the course of the war, Lee would confess to an aide: "I had such implicit confidence in Jackson's skill and energy that I never troubled myself to give him detailed instructions. The most general suggestions were all that he needed." On this occasion, Lee simply traced his finger along the map in a broad direction through the Wilderness and around the Union right flank. Without further explanation, he looked at Jackson and said, "General Stuart will cover your movement with cavalry." A smile beamed across Jackson's face. Standing up and touching the brim of his cap, he stated, "My troops will move at four o'clock."[10]

* * *

Friday, May 1, had been a long day, and Jackson was tired. Since determining the exact route of the flanking maneuver would have to wait until Stuart returned with information on the suitability of the roads, Jackson decided he had time to catch a few hours' sleep before issuing specific orders for the movement. The Confederates had advanced so rapidly on the battle's first day that the headquarters wagon containing Jackson's baggage was still somewhere in the rear, leaving him without a tent or bedroll. So he simply

9   Talcott, "Lee's Strategy at Chancellorsville," 16.

10 *Daily Dispatch* (Richmond, VA), October 26, 1875; Talcott, "Lee's Strategy at Chancellorsville," 16.

leaned his sword against a tree on the edge of the clearing and spread his saddle blanket on the ground under some overhanging pine boughs. Using his saddle as a pillow, the fatigued general lay down for some much-needed rest.

Jackson's assistant adjutant general and chief of staff, Maj. Alexander "Sandie" Pendleton, noticed that Jackson was without a blanket and offered the general his overcoat for a covering. Pendleton—described by a fellow officer as "the most brilliant staff officer in the Army of Northern Virginia"—was a 22-year-old from Lexington, Virginia, who was so close to Jackson that the general reportedly "loved him as a son." Jackson politely refused the use of Pendleton's overcoat, but the young officer persisted, asking the general whether he would at least take the long cape of the coat. Jackson accepted the cape and, using it as a make-shift blanket, stretched out on the ground and fell fast asleep.[11]

The clear spring night was cool and damp, and Jackson awoke two hours later feeling chilled. Getting up to shake off the cold, he noticed a courier had started a small fire in the clearing. He gently laid the borrowed cape over its sleeping owner and walked over to the fire. Along the way he picked up one of several large wooden cracker boxes that littered the area after being discarded by Union soldiers during their retreat the previous day. Placing the box next to the fire, he sat down and tightly closed his coat against the night air. As he warmed himself in front of the flames, Jackson realized that he was suffering the first symptoms of a developing head cold.[12]

Tucker Lacy, who had arrived in camp while Jackson was asleep, also approached the fire, and the general offered him a seat. Lacy initially declined, but, moving over to make room for him on the box, Jackson said, "Sit down. I want to talk to you." Jackson related to his chaplain that Hooker was in a strong position around Chancellorsville, so attacking from the front would "cost a fearful loss." Relying on Lacy's knowledge of the area,

11 Douglas, *I Rode With Stonewall*, 313.

12 Armistead L. Long, *Memoirs of Robert E. Lee* (Secaucus, NJ, 1983), 258; Arthur Rogers, in Dabney-Jackson Collection, box 2, LVA; Peter W. Houck, *Confederate Surgeon: The Personal Recollections of E. A. Craighill* (Lynchburg, VA, 1989), 54; *The Sentinel* (Richmond, VA), May 16, 1863; Douglas, *I Rode With Stonewall*, 220. Douglas states that staff officer James P. Smith was the recipient of the covering, but other accounts relate Jackson placing the cape over its sleeping owner.

Jackson asked, "Do you know of any way by which to flank either their right or left?"[13]

"Yes," Lacy replied. "There is a blind road leading from the furnace and nearly parallel to the Plank Road which falls into a road running northwards, which again leads into the Plank Road three and a half to four miles above Chancellorsville."

Opening one of Hotchkiss' maps, Jackson had Lacy draw the road on paper. "That is too near," he said after studying the route. "It will go within line of the enemy's pickets. Do you know no other?" Lacy did not, but he presumed the Furnace Road itself intersected with the main road somewhere farther to the west, although he had not ridden it. Lacy thought Charles Wellford, the furnace proprietor, would know, and perhaps his son might be able act as a guide. Jackson instructed the pastor to wake Hotchkiss and for the two of them to visit Wellford in order to "ascertain whether those roads meet and are practicable for artillery." Hotchkiss was to return with the information while Lacy secured a guide.[14]

After Lacy and Hotchkiss departed, Jackson was alone again in front of the fire when Col. Armistead L. Long of Lee's personal staff awoke and approached the warmth of the flames. After an exchange of pleasantries, Jackson complained to the colonel of feeling cold. Spotting cooks nearby preparing breakfast, Long walked over and obtained a cup of hot coffee for the appreciative general. As the two officers briefly chatted, the distinctive sound of clanking metal suddenly broke the surrounding quiet. They turned to see that Jackson's sword, which had been leaning against a tree, had fallen over with no apparent cause. Long picked up the sword and handed it to Jackson, who thanked him and buckled it on without comment. The incident, however, immediately disturbed Long, who believed the fallen sword was a bad omen, much like a picture falling off a wall; the memory of the event haunted the colonel throughout the coming day.[15]

Before the break of dawn, Lee also awoke, found another cracker box, and joined Jackson beside the fire. No one knows what conversation passed between the two, but the sight of them sitting alone in front of the fire in the

---

13 Lacy, "Narrative."

14 Ibid.

15 Long, *Memoirs of Lee*, 258.

Engraving depicting the cracker box council between Lee and Jackson.
Battles and Leaders of the Civil War

early morning hours made a lasting impression on the mind of Lt. James Power Smith. An Ohio native and son of a Presbyterian minister, Smith was 25 years old when he began serving as an aide-de-camp to Jackson in 1862. Known as "Jimmy" to the rest of the staff, Smith was a divinity student who had received a degree from the Union Theological Seminary in Hampden Sydney, Virginia, prior to enlisting in the Confederate army. Jackson admired Smith's religious background, calm demeanor, and attention to detail, and he quickly became one of the general's most trusted officers.

Smith was sleeping nearby on a lower slope when the early morning chill awakened him. Turning over, he rubbed his eyes and caught a glimpse of Lee and Jackson sitting on cracker boxes, quietly warming their hands over the small fire. This "cracker box council" between two of the most famous generals of the war would be immortalized in words and pictures for years to come. In 1903, Smith would have a granite marker placed at the site commemorating the location of the Lee-Jackson bivouac.[16]

Around 3:30 a.m., Hotchkiss returned from his visit to Mr. Wellford's house while the two generals were still seated beside the fire. Placing another

16 James P. Smith, "Stonewall Jackson's Last Battle," in *B&L*, vol. 3, pt. 1, 203-214. Smith directed the placement of ten stone markers throughout the area to commemorate various events primarily associated with Lee and Jackson.

cracker box between Lee and Jackson, he spread a map across the top and described a new road Wellford had recently cut southwest through the woods in order to haul cordwood and iron ore to Catharine Furnace. Hotchkiss described how the army could use this rough wagon trail to reach the Brock Road as it traveled north and entered the Plank Road west of the Federal position.

Having previously decided that a flanking march was the intended strategy, Lee and Jackson silently studied the route on the map. Finally, Lee spoke up. "General Jackson, what do you propose to do?"

"Go around here," he replied, tracing his finger along the route drawn by Hotchkiss.

"What do you propose to make this movement with?" Lee asked.

"With my whole corps," Jackson replied without hesitation.

Lee paused for a moment. "What will you leave me?"

"The divisions of Anderson and McLaws," Jackson responded.

Lee paused again. Military tactics dictated that as a commander you should avoid dividing your army in the presence of the enemy, as it provides the adversary with the opportunity of opposing your fractions with his entire force. Lee had already divided his army once at Fredericksburg, and now Jackson was suggesting another large split in front of the enemy. The maneuver would leave Lee with roughly 14,000 men to oppose Hooker's 70,000 while Jackson took his 28,000 men on a 12-mile march around the Union flank. It would be another risky move, with success depending on Hooker staying put around Chancellorsville, expecting Lee to attack from the front.

Lee had always been confident in his ability to read the intentions of the Union commanders, and Hooker was no exception. After a brief and thoughtful reflection, he looked at Jackson and said, "Well, go on."

Lee began writing orders for the movement while Jackson nodded in agreement, with what Hotchkiss described as "an eager smile upon his face." After Lee finished, Jackson stood up, saluted the commanding general, and said, "My troops will move at once, sir."[17]

*   *   *

17 Henderson, *Stonewall Jackson and the American Civil War*, 431-432. Henderson quoted a letter sent to him by Hotchkiss detailing the exchange between Lee and Jackson.

After several delays, including a brief artillery duel, it was actually closer to 7:30 a.m. before the lead elements of Jackson's army began marching down the Catharine Furnace Road. Warm sunshine and a cloudless sky had replaced the morning chill, and Lee stood at the side of the road silently watching the soldiers file past. Jackson, riding Little Sorrel, stopped alongside the commanding general and the two engaged in a brief conversation. Jackson's face was reportedly flushed as he was seen pointing down the road in the direction of his troops. Lee nodded in agreement with something, and Jackson continued his ride west. It would be the last time the two Confederate generals ever saw each other.[18]

The narrow dirt roads winding through the Wilderness forest provided enough room for Jackson's soldiers to march only four abreast, causing a thin column of 28,000 men, artillery, ammunition wagons, and ambulances to be stretched across an arc of ten miles once all the regiments were in motion. Jackson routinely expected his men to maintain a marching pace of two miles an hour, walking for fifty minutes and then resting for ten. On this march, however, the quality of the roads made that speed impossible to maintain. Colonel Porter Alexander described the difficulties of the movement in his memoir: "No one who has ever marched with a long column can form any conception how every little inequality of ground, and every mud hole, especially if the road be narrow, causes a column to string out and lose distance. So that, though the head may advance steadily, the rear has to alternately halt and start, and halt and start, in the most heartbreaking way, wearing out the men and consuming precious daylight."[19]

Jackson spent the morning riding up and down the line prodding the men to stay in formation and continue moving. One officer vividly recalled the scene: "His face was pale, his eyes flashing. Out from his thin, compressed lips came the terse command: 'Press forward, press forward.' In his eagerness, as he rode, he leaned over on the neck of his horse as if in that way the march might be hurried. 'See that the column is kept closed and that there is no straggling,' he more than once ordered, and 'Press on, press on,' was

---

18 Lee, "Chancellorsville," 569-570; Henderson, *Stonewall Jackson and the American Civil War*, 433.

19 Gallagher, *Fighting for the Confederacy*, 201.

repeated again and again." Jackson was otherwise "grave and silent" during the march, with little conversation occurring between him and his staff.[20]

At one point, Old Jack did ride to the front of the column and engage in brief, low-level conversation with Brig. Gen. Robert E. Rodes, whose division was leading the march, Brig. Gen. Raleigh E. Colston, and Col. Thomas Munford of the 2nd Virginia Cavalry, all graduates of the Virginia Military Institute. "I hear it said that General Hooker has more men than he can handle," Jackson remarked. "I should like to have half as many more as I have today, and I should hurl him in the river! The trouble with us has always been to have a reserve to throw in at the critical moment to reap the benefit of advantages gained. We have always had to put in all of our troops and never had enough at the time most needed."[21]

To help maintain secrecy, noise during the march was suppressed as much possible. The soldiers were prohibited from cheering and "strict silence was enforced, the men being allowed to speak only in whispers," according to one North Carolina officer. The difficulty of the terrain combined with temperatures approaching 80 degrees made the going tough for many of the soldiers. "This march was a trying one to the men," Col. C. T. Zachry of the 27th Georgia wrote in his official report. "The day was very warm; many fell out of the ranks exhausted, some fainting and having spasms; only a few had eaten anything since the morning before."[22]

Despite his careful attempts at secrecy and concealment, Jackson's flanking maneuver did not go unnoticed by the Union army. As the troops passed over the small knoll near Catharine Furnace, their march was observed by the Federal outposts on Hazel Grove. Hooker received word shortly after 9:00 a.m. that a large body of Rebel troops had been seen moving west. He was at first uncertain whether this movement represented an attempt to outflank him or the beginning of a Confederate retreat. To be safe, he sent an order to Maj. Gen. Oliver O. Howard, whose XI Corps occupied the right flank, to guard against a possible attack from that

20 Hunter H. McGuire, "Career and Character of General T. J. Jackson," in *SHSP* (1897), vol. 25, 110; Gallagher, *Fighting for the Confederacy*, 201-202.

21 Robertson, *Stonewall Jackson: The Man, The Soldier, The Legend*, 718.

22 V. E. Turner and H. C. Hall, "Twenty-third Regiment," in Walter Clark, ed., *Histories of Regiments from North Carolina*, 5 vols. (Raleigh, NC, 1901), vol. 2, 228; *OR* 25, pt. 2, 981.

direction. Unfortunately for Hooker and his army, the order went largely unheeded.

At noon, after the Confederate march was well underway, Hooker ordered Maj. Gen. Daniel E. Sickles to "advance cautiously" and to "harass the movement as much as possible." Sharp fighting near the furnace between Sickles' men and a regiment of Georgia infantry left to guard the column's flank began around 12:30 p.m. Nearer to the furnace, the Union troops could plainly see the Confederate column turn south as it marched along a bend in the road. This limited observation reinforced the idea of a Confederate retreat—an idea Hooker was more than willing to accept. After Sickles' attack failed to stop Jackson's movement, Hooker issued an order at 2:30 p.m. to prepare for an early morning pursuit of the "retreating" Confederates.[23]

Jackson and the head of his corps reached the junction of the Brock and Orange Plank roads at 2:00 p.m., just as the tail of the column was passing Catharine Furnace. His original intention had been to turn east on the Plank Road and attack the end of the unsuspecting Federal line. But within moments of his arrival at the junction, Brig. Gen. Fitz Lee, whose cavalry force had led the flanking march, rode up with news of a recent discovery. "General," he said excitedly, "if you will ride with me, halting your column here, out of sight, I will show you the enemy's right, and you will perceive the great advantage of attacking down the Old Turnpike instead of the Plank Road, the enemy's lines being taken in reverse."[24]

Jackson and a single courier followed Lee through the woods to the top of a hill overlooking the Federal line. From there, Jackson could plainly see Union soldiers about a half mile away—completely oblivious to the threat before them. Their arms were stacked as they smoked, chatted, and played cards. To the left, Jackson could see the Talley farmhouse and the fork between the Old Turnpike and the Orange Plank Road in front of Wilderness Church. To the right, he saw Dowdall's Tavern, the homestead of the son of the founder of Chancellorsville.

Jackson stared intently through his binoculars for five minutes without uttering a word, even though his lips were silently moving the entire time.

---

23 *OR* 25, pt. 1, 386; Bigelow, *Chancellorsville*, 289.

24 Lee, "Chancellorsville," 572.

Fitz Lee was convinced the devout Jackson was speaking to the "Great God of Battles."

The young cavalry officer's analysis of the tactical situation was correct. The Union line stretched farther west than anticipated, so attacking down the Plank Road would put Jackson's forces in front of the Union army instead of on its flank. The Confederates would need to swing left an additional mile and a half and strike the Yankee right from along the turnpike. Turning suddenly to the courier, Jackson ordered, "Tell General Rodes to move across the Plank Road and halt when he gets to the Old Turnpike. I will join him there."[25]

Jackson took one final look at the Federal position and, without acknowledging or thanking Lee, turned his horse and galloped down the hill back to the Brock Road.

"When he came back from the view," Porter Alexander noted, "there was a perceptible eagerness in his air and he hurried the head of the column over to a cross road we had to follow from there." Jackson then dismounted, sat on a stump by the side of the road, and wrote his last dispatch:

Near 3 P.M.

May 2d, 1863

General,
The enemy has made a stand at Chancellor's which is about two miles from Chancellorsville. I hope as soon as practicable to attack.

I trust that an ever kind Providence will bless us with great success.

Respectfully,
T. J. JACKSON
Lt. Genl.

Genl. R. E. Lee

The leading division is up & the next two appear to be well closed.
T. J. J.[26]

---

25 Ibid.

26 Gallagher, *Fighting for the Confederacy*, 202; Smith, "Stonewall Jackson's Last Battle," 206. The original copy of the last dispatch is in the Library of Virginia in Richmond.

Jack Haydon, a local resident who had acted as one of the guides through the countryside, had completed his task once the army arrived at the crossroads. After Jackson dismissed him, Haydon asked the general if he would do him a favor.

"What is it, sir?" Jackson curtly responded.

"Take care of yourself," Haydon replied.[27]

Upon reaching the Old Turnpike, the column turned right and marched east for nearly a mile before stopping along a low ridge just beyond the farm of John R. Luckett. Jackson deployed the men three divisions deep across a line that stretched for three-quarters of a mile on each side of the turnpike. Except for those in the cleared area around the Luckett farm, most of the men were concealed in the thick Wilderness. Another two hours of daylight would pass before the entire Second Corps was fully in line and ready to attack.

As the divisions were falling into line, a former student of Jackson's at VMI, Capt. Marcellus N. Moorman, commanding a battery of artillery attached to the cavalry, approached Jackson to clarify whether his men were to remain with the infantry or withdraw with the cavalry. "Captain," Jackson answered his old pupil, "I will give you the honor of going in on my front line." Shortly thereafter, heavy artillery firing could be heard far to the east, and Moorman asked Jackson whom he thought it could be. "How far do you suppose it is?" he asked the captain.

"Five or six miles," Moorman replied.

"I suppose it is General Lee," Jackson said. "Time we are moving." According to plan, Lee was making demonstrations in the Union front to occupy Hooker's attention and prevent him from sending troops to the right flank.[28]

Jackson's directions for the attack were clear. The entire line was to push forward to the Talley farm, using the turnpike as a guide. After taking the heights at Talley's, the force was to proceed toward the second objective,

---

27 Murray F. Taylor, letter to *CV* magazine, Jan. 13, 1904, Thomas J. Jackson Collection, Museum of the Confederacy (MOC), 3. An edited version of the letter appears in *CV* (October 1904), 492-494.

28 Marcellus N. Moorman, "Narrative of Events," in *SHSP* (1902), vol. 30, 111; Marcellus Moorman to Hunter H. McGuire, April 8, 1898, Hotchkiss Papers, reel 15, Library of Congress (LC).

Dowdall's Tavern; under no circumstances was there to be any pause in the advance.[29]

Jackson sat on his horse near the Luckett farmhouse and glanced up and down the line of Confederate gray. Inspired by the sight of the many VMI graduates he noticed among his staff, he proudly announced to those around: "The Institute will be heard from today."[30]

The atmosphere around the farm was much like the calm before an approaching storm. When told the final preparations were complete, Jackson looked at his watch. It was 5:15 p.m. With the evening sun setting at his back, Jackson calmly asked his division commander, "Are you ready, General Rodes?"

"Yes, sir," Rodes answered emphatically.

Launching the greatest attack of his military career, Stonewall Jackson quietly replied, "You can go forward, then."[31]

29 *OR* 25, pt. 1, 940-941.

30 Robertson, *Stonewall Jackson: The Man, The Soldier, The Legend*, 721.

31 Smith, "Stonewall Jackson's Last Battle," 208.

Chapter Four

They Never Run Too Fast

the evening sun set behind the Wilderness thicket, the Union soldiers of Maj. Gen. Oliver O. Howard's XI Corps were leisurely sitting around campfires cooking dinner and listening to a regimental band, when their attention was suddenly drawn to a deer that bounded through the Federal camp. An entertaining chase ensued as several soldiers quickly ran after the animal in a vain attempt to catch it. Those watching the amusing footrace were surprised when a second deer unexpectedly bolted past them. Looking toward the Wilderness, they were astonished to see numerous wild animals charge out of the brush and into the open field.

What the men of the XI Corps did not know at the time was that Jackson's advance had begun beyond the edge of the woodlands, and "its first lively effects," General Howard wrote, "appeared in the startled rabbits, squirrels, quail, and other wild game flying wildly hither and thither in evident terror, and escaping, where possible, into adjacent clearings."[1]

---

1 Oliver O. Howard, "The Eleventh Corps at Chancellorsville," in *B&L*, vol. 3, pt. 1, 197.

The arrival of the terrified animals was quickly followed by the cracking sound of musketry as the few Union pickets stationed in the woods began firing at an advancing mass of Confederate gray. The next sound that emerged from the bushes was unmistakable to veteran Yankee soldiers, but one many of the new men in the regiments were hearing for the first time: "that demonical huntsman cry" known as the "Rebel Yell." As one Union colonel recalled, the roar from the woods broke forth "so suddenly upon the stillness of a summer afternoon and so unexpectantly, that it almost chilled my blood."[2]

Jackson's men, although bleeding and tattered from the thick briers of the Wilderness, flowed forth from the woods like an avalanche. The surprise was so overwhelming that Union Maj. Gen. Carl Schurz said the entire Yankee line was "rolled up and swept away in a moment." Confederate General Robert Rodes described the chaotic scene in his official report: "So complete was the success of the whole maneuver, and such was the surprise of the enemy, that scarcely any organized resistance was met with after the first volley was fired. They fled in the wildest confusion, leaving the field strewn with arms, accouterments, clothing, caissons, and field pieces in every direction."[3]

As the attack progressed, desperately hungry Confederates took the opportunity to "pluck and eat" by pausing momentarily at campfires to steal part of a cooking dinner or to take a drink of real coffee before renewing their chase of the fleeing Yankees. Small pockets of Union resistance did spring up, but none were able to stem the Rebel tide.

Hearing the clash of muskets, General Howard rode up from his headquarters at Dowdall's Tavern to discover his troops in "a blind panic and great confusion." In an act of personal courage, he grabbed an abandoned Union flag and rode headlong into the fight, attempting to rally his men, but to no avail. The men of his corps would not regroup until three hours later, after they had scurried to the other side of Chancellorsville two and a half miles to the east.[4]

---

2   George C. Eggleston, *A Captain in the Ranks: A Romance of Affairs* (New York, NY, 1904), 7; Ed Malles, ed., *Bridge Building in Wartime: Colonel Wesley Brainerd's Memoir of the 50th New York Volunteer Engineers* (Knoxville, TN, 1997), 141.

3   *OR* 25, pt. 1, 655, 941.

4   Ibid., 630.

An 1865 photograph of Dowdall's Tavern.
Library of Congress

The Confederates achieved their first objective of Talley's Farm within half an hour of beginning the attack and quickly continued their drive toward the second at Dowdall's Tavern. Just east of the tavern, Union forces under the command of Col. Adolphus Buschbeck attempted a gallant stand along a line of rifle pits facing west and extending to each side of the Plank Road. His position being easily outflanked after a brief fight, this "Buschbeck Line" was also forced to withdraw toward Chancellorsville with the rest of the Union forces.

As his troops raced eastward "with the velocity of a meteor and the fury of a thunderstorm," Stonewall Jackson rode closely behind, relentlessly encouraging his men to continue their pursuit. Every few minutes, one staff officer recalled, he would repeat the order "Press forward! Press forward!" as he leaned over and extended a hand beyond his horse's head, "as if he was trying to push forward the column with his hand."[5]

At one point, an excited young officer ran up, shouting, "General, they are running too fast for us; we can't come up with them."

"They never run too fast for me, sir," Jackson tersely replied.[6]

Captain Richard E. Wilbourn, Jackson's chief signal officer, had never seen the general as pleased with success as he was that evening. "He was in unusually fine spirits," Wilbourn wrote in a letter, "and every time he heard the cheering of our men which is ever the signal of victory—he raised his right hand a few seconds as if in acknowledgement of the blessing and to return thanks to God for the victory."[7]

Pausing occasionally to say a prayer over dead Confederate soldiers along the road, Jackson continued his own pursuit of the retreating Federal army. A battery of horse artillery under the direction of Maj. Robert F. Beckham was on the Plank Road maintaining a continuous fire in support of

---

5 C. C. Sanders, "Battle of Chancellorsville," in *SHSP* (1901), vol. 29, 169; Richard E. Wilbourn to Robert Dabney, December 12, 1863, in Charles William Dabney Papers, Southern Historical Collection (SHC), University of North Carolina.

6 William F. Randolph, "General Jackson's Mortal Wound," in *SHSP* (1901), vol. 29, 332.

7 Richard E. Wilbourn to Charles Faulkner, May 1863, in Charles J. Faulkner Papers, Virginia Historical Society (VHS).

the advance when Jackson rode up to the surprised officer. "Young man, I congratulate you," Jackson said as he shook Beckham's hand.[8]

*   *   *

Two miles to the east of Stonewall Jackson's position, Joe Hooker and two staff members were sitting on the veranda of the Chancellor house around 6:30 p.m. enjoying the spring evening. Due to an odd acoustical shadow, sounds from the hour-long struggle on his right flank never reached Hooker's location. As the three officers chatted, something to the west caught the attention of Capt. Harry Russell. Stepping off the porch, he took out his binoculars and gazed down the Plank Road. "My God!" he exclaimed, "Here they come!"[9]

Running down the road was a stampede of men, horses, and mules from the broken XI Corps. Hooker and his officers jumped on their horses and rode into the melee in a vain attempt to stop the flight. Assuming the Confederate army was on the heels of his retreating forces, Hooker ordered the III Corps, held in reserve near the Chancellor house, into the breach.

In a short two hours' time on the evening of May 2, 1863, Jackson's army had managed to surprise 12,000 soldiers anchoring the Union right flank and drive them back nearly two miles toward Chancellorsville. But as the light faded with the setting sun, the Confederate assault began to lose steam. The speed of the advance combined with the dense entanglement of the Wilderness had led to as much disorder among the attackers as it had in the Union army. The two Confederate forces leading the attack, Robert Rodes' division in front and Brig. Gen. Raleigh E. Colston's in back, had become "mingled together in inextricable confusion."[10]

An unexpected appearance by the 8th Pennsylvania cavalry also added to the chaos of the situation. Stationed near the Union artillery position at Hazel Grove, men in the unit were leisurely playing cards, since the sounds

---

8 Henry B. McClellan, *The Life and Campaigns of Major-General J. E. B. Stuart* (Boston, MA, 1885), 234.

9 Augustus C. Hamlin, *The Battle of Chancellorsville: The Attack of Stonewall Jackson and his Army Upon the Right Flank of the Army of the Potomac at Chancellorsville, Virginia, on Saturday Afternoon, May 2, 1863* (Bangor, ME, 1896), 51.

10 *OR* 25, pt. 1, 941.

of the fight to the west had not reached them through the thick woods. Ordered to report to General Howard, the men mounted and slowly rode up the Hazel Grove Road toward the Plank Road, completely unaware that the position toward which they were heading had been overrun by the Confederates.

Reaching the main road, the members of the lead element abruptly found themselves surrounded by Rebel soldiers. The path being too narrow to turn the column around, the men had no choice but to continue forward. "Draw sabers and charge!" shouted the commanding officer. A "perfect frenzy of excitement" then ensued as the Pennsylvanians galloped for safety. "The enemy were as thick as bees," another officer recalled. "We were in columns of fours and on the dead run, and when we struck the enemy there occurred a 'jam' of living and dead men, friends and enemies, and horses, and the weight of the rear of our squadron broke us into utter confusion, so that at the moment every man was for himself." Although the Confederates suffered few casualties from the charge, the encounter caused a warning to go out to be prepared for surprise attacks by enemy cavalry.[11]

At 7:15 p.m., Rodes finally halted the attack. "Such was the confusion and the darkness that it was not deemed advisable to make a farther advance," he explained in his official report. The Rebel soldiers were also exhausted and hungry. In one day they had marched 12 miles around the enemy flank, and had followed that with a two-mile chase of the Union army through the woods and fields around Chancellorsville. Rodes sent word to Jackson asking him to send forward Maj. Gen. Ambrose P. Hill's division, currently in the rear, to continue the advance while his men regrouped.[12]

A. P. Hill, who went by his middle name of "Powell," was Jackson's best divisional commander. He was known for wearing a black slouch hat and calico shirts made by his wife. Despite his fine capabilities as a general, Hill and Jackson had a contentious working relationship. Jackson's strict sense of military order (he once instructed an officer, "You must obey my orders first and reason about them afterwards") clashed with Hill's tendency toward "being too quick to resent a seeming overstepping of authority," as Hotchkiss described him. Their animosity reached a crescendo after the

---

11 Pennock Huey and Andrew Wells, "The Charge of the Eighth Pennsylvania Cavalry," in *B&L*, vol. 3, pt. 1, 186-188.

12 *OR* 25, pt. 1, 941.

battle of Second Manassas in 1862 when Jackson had Hill placed under arrest on a charge of "Neglect of Duty." Hill, who once referred to Jackson as "that crazy old Presbyterian fool," then filed countercharges against Jackson. It would take Lee's direct involvement in a meeting between them before the charges were dropped on both sides.[13]

Jackson was near Dowdall's Tavern, sending couriers to artillery and infantry units with orders to continue the advance, when he received Rodes' message that the attack had been halted. Sending orders for Hill to move rapidly ahead and relieve Rodes, Jackson rode off for the front, determined to resume the attack on the fleeing Federals. "General Jackson and staff came thundering down the road by us," remembered Roland S. Williams of the 13th North Carolina Regiment. "Press the enemy until night-fall!" Jackson shouted as he went past.[14]

Arriving at the front, Jackson witnessed firsthand the extent of the confusion and disorganization in the Confederate forces. "Men, get into line, get into line!" he shouted as he rode among the units. "Whose command is this? Colonel, get your men instantly in line!"[15]

He eventually found General Rodes, who was obviously pleased with his men's performance. "General Jackson," Rodes beamed, "[m]y division behaved splendidly this evening and you must give them a big name in your report."

"I shall take great pleasure in doing so, and I congratulate you and your command for it," Jackson replied as he continued his ride forward.[16]

Positioned a quarter of a mile south on the Hazel Grove Road, Maj. Norvell Cobb of the 44th Virginia Regiment took a squad of men forward into the woods to reconnoiter during the lull in the attack while the Confederate units reorganized. Just beyond a line of log earthworks that had been abandoned by the Union army, Cobb encountered a large group of

13 J. William Jones, "Stonewall Jackson: Personal Reminiscences and Anecdotes of his Character," in *SHSP* (1891), 155; Hotchkiss, *Make Me a Map of the Valley*, 87; James I. Robertson, *General A. P. Hill: The Story of a Confederate Warrior* (New York, NY, 1987), 157; Douglas, *I Rode with Stonewall*, 195; "Unveiling of the Statue of General Ambrose Powell Hill at Richmond, Virginia, May 30, 1892," in *SHSP* (1892), vol. 20, 385.

14 R. S. Williams, "Thirteenth Regiment," in Walter Clark, ed., *Histories of the Several Regiments*, vol. 1, 667.

15 Norvell Cobb, "Memorandum," in Dabney-Jackson Collection, box 2, LVA.

16 Richard E. Wilbourn to Robert Dabney, December 12, 1863.

Federal soldiers who immediately surrendered to his small force without a fight. While marching the prisoners to the rear, the major happened upon Jackson trying to organize troops near an old schoolhouse at the junction of the Hazel Grove and Plank roads. Cobb stopped for a moment to inform the general of the abandoned works he had discovered in the woods. The works extended south, paralleling the Union line, and consisted of log barricades with abattis (a line of sharpened sticks set in the ground with points outward) on the western side.

"Major," Jackson replied, "I need your help a while, this disorder must be corrected. Find General Rodes and tell him to occupy that barricade with his troops. Then go along the right and tell the troops from me, to get into line and preserve the order."[17]

The lead elements of Hill's division rushing forward to relieve Rodes' exhausted troops were a brigade of North Carolina soldiers led by Brig. Gen. James H. Lane. Small in stature but large in fighting spirit, Lane was a Virginia native who had graduated from VMI and taught military tactics at the institution before leaving prior to the outbreak of the war to become an instructor at the North Carolina Military Institute. As Lane's men were marching to the front down the congested Plank Road, a sudden, unexpected artillery barrage from the Union side sent them running for cover into the adjacent woods.

The cascade of shells into the Confederate ranks was the result of an action by Jackson's former pupil, Capt. Marcellus Moorman, who had charged his horse artillery forward with Rodes' initial assault. Moorman's three cannon were advanced and unlimbered in the middle of the Plank Road just before an important intersection with the Bullock Road to the north and another path from Hazel Grove to the south.

The Bullock Road stretched northeasterly from the Plank Road toward the U.S. Ford. Sixty-five yards north of its origin from the Plank Road, it crossed a more narrow and isolated dirt path known as the Mountain Road. Traveling east, the Mountain Road ran parallel to the Plank Road for approximately half a mile before curving down and connecting back to the main road nearly half a mile west of the Chancellor house. A road from Hazel Grove also entered the Plank Road opposite the start of the Bullock Road and was one of three outlets from the farm to the main road. The

17 Cobb, "Memorandum."

primary route from the grove connected with the Plank Road one and a half miles west of Chancellorsville at the location of the old schoolhouse. South of the old schoolhouse, two branches split off the main trunk, one path running northeast and entering the Plank Road at the intersection where Moorman had his artillery, and another traveling northwest and emerging at the corner of a field east of Dowdall's Tavern.[18]

While Lane's men were moving to the front to relieve Rodes, Moorman fired his three guns in the direction of the Union lines. His shots were immediately answered by 37 Federal cannon posted three-quarters of a mile away on a cleared elevation around the Fairview homestead, slightly west of Chancellorsville. The massive Union response sent Lane's men scrambling for cover and brought an abrupt halt to the Confederate reorganization.

Noticing that the deployment had ceased, A. P. Hill sent his adjutant, Maj. William H. Palmer, to inquire about the reason for Lane's delay. Lane told Palmer he was not eager to lose his command during an attempt to form a line in dark woods under a "terrific and murderous artillery fire." Lane thought the Union fire was simply a response to the Confederate artillery, and if the Rebels stopped firing, so too would the Yankees. Palmer relayed the message to Hill, who ordered the firing to cease and, as Lane predicted, the Union shelling also stopped.[19]

With the artillery now quiet, Lane proceeded to form his men into line of battle. He stretched the 33rd North Carolina regiment across the Plank Road and sent the men forward as skirmishers past an unfinished building known as the Van Wert house, a small, wood-frame structure located on the south side of the road. At the intersection of the Bullock and Plank roads, Lane deployed the 7th and 37th North Carolina regiments south of the road and the 28th and 18th North Carolina regiments to the left, or north side, of the

---

18 The presence of the road from Hazel Grove opposite the Bullock Road intersection has been ignored by most modern battlefield references. Its existence is confirmed through several primary sources, period battlefield maps, and a 1932 U.S. Geological survey map of the Chancellorsville battlefield. See David Kyle to A. C. Hamlin, November 8, 1894, in A. C. Hamlin Collection (ACHC), Harvard University; James M. Talley to A. C. Hamlin, June 1, 1892, in ACHC, Harvard University; James H. Lane to A. C. Hamlin, August 31, 1892, in ACHC, Harvard University; William H. Palmer, "Another Account of It," in *CV* (May 1905); "Topographic Maps of Chancellorsville and Salem Church Battlefields, Spotsylvania County, Virginia," U.S. Department of the Interior, 1932, LC.

19 James H. Lane to A. C. Hamlin, August 31, 1892; James H. Lane to Marcellus Moorman, April 22, 1898, in Hotchkiss Papers, reel 15, LC.

Plank Road. The right end of the 18th and the left end of the 37th rested on the road.[20]

Back near the old schoolhouse, Jackson was continuing his ride to the front when he was stopped by a courier delivering a message from Jeb Stuart. Private David J. Kyle of the 9th Virginia Cavalry handed Jackson a large, sealed envelope, and sat quietly on his horse as the general read the dispatch. Kyle was a 19-year-old local boy who, before the war, had lived in the Bullock farmhouse located on the road that bore its name. After reading the message, Jackson looked at Kyle and asked the young private whether he knew the surrounding country. Kyle assured him he did, to which Jackson replied, "You keep along with me."[21]

Jackson, accompanied by his staff and several couriers, quickly rode to the intersection where his new battle line was forming. Lane, who had just finished deploying his men, was on the Plank Road calling out in the darkness for A. P. Hill. Recognizing Lane's voice, Jackson asked what he wanted. The brigadier said he was looking to obtain further orders from Hill, but since Jackson was present, he would ask him. "Push right ahead, Lane," Jackson responded, while simultaneously gesturing with his right hand in a pushing motion toward the enemy. After ordering the 28th and 18th North Carolina to move forward a short distance, Lane proceeded down the right side of the line to advance his other two regiments while Jackson continued his ride forward.[22]

Jackson had ridden ahead only a short distance when he encountered Hill and his staff on the Plank Road. The impatient Jackson asked his divisional commander how long it would be until he was ready to advance. Hill answered but a few more moments, as he was just then finishing the

20 *OR* 25, pt. 1, 916; James H. Lane to Marcellus Moorman, April 22, 1898. The Van Wert house, also described in various accounts as the Van Wart building, the unfinished church, or the unfinished house, is an important landmark in the story of Jackson's wounding. The structure did not survive the war and its precise location is unknown. It is believed to have been located at a site opposite the current Chancellorsville Battlefield Visitor's Center and under the pavement of the eastbound lanes of Route 3. See Harrison, *Chancellorsville Battlefield Sites*, 89-93.

21 David J. Kyle, manuscript for *CV* (1895), bound volume 207, Fredericksburg and Spotsylvania National Military Park (FSNMP). An edited version appears as "Jackson's Guide When Shot," in *CV* (September 1896), 308-309.

22 *OR* 25, pt. 1, 916; James H. Lane to A. C. Hamlin, August 31, 1892; James H. Lane to Marcellus Moorman, April 22, 1898.

relief of Rodes. Jackson also asked Hill whether he was familiar with the road from Chancellorsville to the U.S. Ford. "I have not travelled over it for many years," Hill responded, saying a guide, if available, would be helpful.

"Captain Boswell," Jackson said as he turned toward his chief engineer, "report to General Hill." Then, staring back at Hill, he directed, "When you reach Chancellorsville, allow nothing to stop you. Press on to the United States Ford."[23]

North of the road, the 18th North Carolina regiment had completed a short advance toward the Confederate skirmish line and was now in a position alongside the forward location of Jackson and Hill on the Plank Road. The men and officers of the 18th regiment never noticed as Jackson and his escort quietly left that spot and continued ahead down the Plank Road, followed a few moments later by Hill and his staff.[24]

23 Taylor to *CV*, January 13, 1904.

24 *OR* 25, pt. 1, 916; William H. McLaurin, "Eighteenth Regiment," in Walter Clark, ed., *Histories of the Several Regiments*, vol. 2, 37. Since the time of Jackson's wounding, debate has occurred over whether Jackson reconnoitered down the Plank Road or along the Mountain Road to the north. See Appendix I for a detailed analysis of the controversy.

Chapter Five

My Arm Is Broken

It was close to 9:00 p.m. on May 2, 1863, when Jackson and his escort slowly rode down the Orange Plank Road, beyond the main Confederate line that was forming behind them. Although the night was too dark to distinctly recognize individuals at a distance, the pale light of an almost full moon was enough to silhouette riders along the open road. With the pause in battle, the sounds of cracking muskets and booming artillery had been replaced by the surrounding cry of whippoorwills. "I think there must have been ten thousand," one officer would later remark.[1]

Knowing that he had skirmishers out in front, Jackson thought it was safe to continue his ride ahead and scout for a nighttime attack. To his left was Capt. Richard E. Wilbourn, chief signal officer of the Second Corps. "The enemy had been driven from the field entirely," Wilbourn recalled, "and it was not known certainly whether they were still retreating or had made another stand and were trying to rally their discomforted columns."

Born in Mississippi, Wilbourn had been wounded in the right arm at the battle of Second Manassas in 1862, and the 24-year-old officer still did not

---

1 "The Death of Stonewall Jackson," *Daily Richmond Whig*, October 7, 1865.

have full strength in the extremity. Traveling in a column of twos behind Jackson and Wilbourn were the rest of the escort: Capt. William F. Randolph, in charge of couriers; Lt. Joseph G. Morrison, Jackson's brother-in-law and aide-de-camp; Sgt. William E. Cunliffe, signal corps; Pvt. W. T. Wynn, signal corps; Pvt. Joshua O. Johns, courier; Pvt. Lloyd T. Smith, courier; and Pvt. David Kyle, courier.[2]

As the group made its way ever closer to the Union line, one reluctant staff officer asked, "General, don't you think this is the wrong place for you?"

"The danger is all over," Jackson quickly snapped. "The enemy is routed. Go back and tell A. P. Hill to press right on."[3]

Hill and his staff were about 50 yards behind Jackson and had slowly started following the corps commander as his group rode forward. Riding with Hill were: Maj. William H. Palmer, assistant adjutant; Capt. Boswell of Jackson's staff; Capt. Conway R. Howard, chief engineer; Capt. Benjamin W. Leigh, volunteer aide-de-camp; Capt. James F. Forbes, volunteer aide-de-camp; Lt. Murray F. Taylor, aide-de-camp; Sgt. George W. Tucker, chief courier; Pvt. Richard J. Muse, courier; and Pvt. Eugene L. Saunders, courier.[4]

Jackson continued riding down the Plank Road before coming to a halt at the side of the road just short of the skirmishers and about 100 yards beyond the line of Lane's 18th North Carolina. He sat motionless on Little Sorrel as he listened to noises emanating from the Union line some 250 yards away. The remote sounds of men chopping trees and digging trenches

---

2 Richard E. Wilbourn to Robert Dabney, December 12, 1863; Joseph G. Morrison to Spier Whitaker, June 27, 1900, VHS; Richard E. Wilbourn to Jubal A. Early, March 3, 1873, Jubal Anderson Early Papers, vol. 6, LC; Richard E. Wilbourn to Charles Faulkner, May 1863; Philip A. Bruce, ed., *History of Virginia*, 6 vols. (Chicago, IL, 1924), vol. 5, 286; Kyle, "Jackson's Guide When Shot," 308. All members of Jackson's escort are documented by others as being on the reconnaissance except for Kyle and Smith. These individuals self-report their presence and are not mentioned in other accounts. In two separate accounts, a Jackson courier with the last name of "Shearer" or "Sherrer" is also mentioned as being in the vicinity during the event, but his exact identity is unknown.

3 *Daily Richmond Whig*, October 7, 1865.

4 Benjamin W. Leigh to wife, May 12, 1863, in Dabney-Jackson Collection, box 1, LVA; Palmer, "Another Account of It," 232. On an undated map William Palmer drew for Hamlin, he also listed a courier with the last name "Kirkpatrick" as being present and killed during the event. See ACHC, Harvard University.

indicated that the Yankees had stopped running and were now building defenses to oppose a Confederate attack. Other than the distant echoes from the Yankee lines and the singing of the mournful whippoorwills, "All was quiet," Wilbourn remarked, "[t]he enemy having in the darkness of the night, disappeared entirely from our sight."[5]

To the rear and south of Jackson's position, however, an unfortunate series of events was unfolding that would drastically alter the course of the evening.

The Confederate front line was in a heightened state of alert after General Lane had cautioned his commanders during deployment to keep a close watch, since they were the lead element of the army and a nighttime advance was expected. South of the Plank Road, Lane was just about to give an order for the 7th and 37th North Carolina regiments to advance when an officer from the 7th approached the general and requested a momentary delay. Noises had been heard in the woods on the far right, and the officer thought it prudent to first investigate whether the sounds indicated the enemy was closer than originally believed.

As the two Confederate officers discussed the situation, soldiers from the 7th North Carolina arrived with Union Lt. Col. Levi H. Smith of the 128th Pennsylvania holding a stick tied with a white handkerchief.[6]

Having been under orders to re-occupy the log earthworks abandoned during the retreat earlier in the day, Smith had unknowingly advanced his men between the skirmishers of the 33rd North Carolina in front and the main Confederate line in formation south of the Plank Road. Finding the barricade already occupied, he was unable to tell in the dark whether the soldiers were friend or foe, so he approached the line with a flag of truce asking who was present. Promptly captured by the Confederates, he was taken up the line to meet Lane.

An indignant Smith demanded to be set free, claiming that his intention had been not to surrender but merely to ascertain who controlled the field. However, in Lane's opinion, the action was an illegitimate use of the white flag, so he refused to release Smith unless he received orders to the contrary

5   Richard E. Wilbourn to Robert Dabney, December 12, 1863.

6   *OR* 25, pt. 1, 916.

from General Hill. Lane also sent Lt. James W. Emack and four men to reconnoiter the woods ahead in search of more Federal troops.

Emack and his men had proceeded only a short distance when they stumbled upon 200 soldiers of Smith's 128th Pennsylvania infantry who were awaiting the return of their commander. Drawing his sword, the quick-thinking lieutenant announced, "Men, Jackson has surrounded you; down with your guns, else we will shoot the last one of you!" Confused and startled, the entire regiment immediately surrendered, and Emack marched the group back to the log works. Smith was still attempting to "argufy" the circumstances of his capture with Lane when Emack arrived with the commander's surrendered regiment.[7]

Farther ahead in the dark woods, another bewildered Union officer was approaching the far right of the 33rd North Carolina skirmishers. Brigadier General Joseph F. Knipe, commanding the Federal brigade to which the 128th Pennsylvania was attached, rode in front of the Confederate skirmish line and called out for General Williams, his divisional commander. A sergeant of the Rebel picket, hearing the brigadier shout for a Union general, assumed he was an enemy officer and fired a single shot in Knipe's direction. This lone firing in the direction of the Federal line triggered a return volley from Union pickets a short distance ahead in the woods. The Confederate skirmishers fired back, initiating a cascade of volleys from both sides.[8]

With the opposing pickets south of the Plank Road trading shots, the jittery 7th and 37th North Carolina regiments, believing more enemy forces were to their front, blindly unleashed their own volley into the woods. Soldiers of the 33rd North Carolina had to dive to the ground for cover as they suddenly found themselves in a cross-fire from front and back. Union pickets were quickly placed in a similar predicament as the main Federal line behind them opened up in response to the Confederate fire. Like a chain reaction, the shooting began rolling up the main Confederate line from right to left, and artillery captain Marcellus Moorman found himself under fire.

Moorman and his cannon were still in their advanced position in the middle of the Plank Road as soldiers of the 37th North Carolina to the right

---

7   Ibid.; Moorman, "Narrative of Events," 113; James H. Lane to A. C. Hamlin, August 31, 1892.

8   Ibid.; James H. Lane to Marcellus Moorman, April 22, 1898.

of the road sent a volley in their direction. His startled artillery horses turned and ran for the rear as Moorman rushed toward the line, shouting, "What are you firing at? Are you trying to kill all my men in front of you? There are no Yankees here!" The firing ceased for a moment, and Moorman returned to his guns. There he noticed Jackson and his escort riding back from the front and into the woods north of the road.[9]

Jackson and his staff had been sitting silently on their horses listening to the activity in the Union lines when the solitary gunshot at Knipe prompted the Union pickets to fire and subsequently brought responses from the Confederate skirmish line. Once the opposing pickets began exchanging volleys, Jackson's group turned around and rode west on the Plank Road back toward the Confederate lines. The subsequent fire from the 37th North Carolina that had threatened Moorman also whizzed past Jackson and his escort as they were returning along the same path. Using the woods for cover, Jackson's group left the open road and entered the brush to their right while continuing their westward ride.

The picket firing had also prompted Gen. A. P. Hill and his staff to turn around; now, instead of trailing Jackson, they were the lead group as the two parties rode back to the line and through the woods on the northern edge of the Plank Road. Just ahead of them, concealed in the thick brush, were the vigilant and anxious men of Lane's 18th North Carolina Regiment. With each group unaware of the other's location, the fog of war was about to change the course of Civil War history.

*   *   *

With the right end of its line resting on the edge of the Plank Road, the 18th North Carolina stretched north into the tangled thicket of the Wilderness. Many soldiers in the Confederate unit were still using the older, smoothbore musket that fired a .69 caliber round ball with an effective range of about 100 yards. The men of the regiment had heard the fighting erupt south of the road and were anticipating it would reach them. "We were never

9   OR 25, pt. 1, 922; Spier Whitaker, "The Wounding of Jackson," in Walter Clark, ed., *Histories of Regiments from North Carolina*, vol. 5, 97-98; William L. Hollis to Hunter H. McGuire, May 16, 1896, Thomas J. Jackson Collection, MOC; Moorman, "Narrative of Events," 114; Marcellus Moorman to Hunter McGuire, April 8, 1898.

Battle flag carried by the 18th North Carolina Regiment at Chancellorsville.
The flag was captured by Union forces on May 3, 1863.
Courtesy North Carolina Museum of History

more on the alert and wide awake than that night," William H. McLaurin of
the 18th wrote.[10]

It was around 9:30 p.m. when the stillness surrounding them was
suddenly disturbed by the sounds of approaching horses. Hill and Jackson,
still leading separate groups, were drawing near the line of battle. To the
anxious men of the 18th, the clatter of nearly 20 riders coming through the
woods from the front had all the markings of an assault. As Hill's group
came within 20 yards of the regiment, the sight of the silhouetted horsemen

10 McLaurin, "Eighteenth Regiment," 38.

prompted someone to shout, "Yankee cavalry!" Instinctively, the entire line unleashed a volley into the moonlit forest.[11]

The sudden crack and blaze of musketry wreaked havoc among the riders ahead in the woods. Horses reared and bolted from the scene as bullets indiscriminately struck both men and animals. A. P. Hill's staff, the group closest to the firing, "disappeared as if stricken by lightening," said Benjamin Leigh. Private Saunders was killed instantly and the other courier, Muse, received two gunshots in the face. Captain Forbes was mortally wounded and would die later at a field hospital. Leigh struck his head on the ground after being thrown from his wounded horse. Palmer's horse was killed from under him and Tucker was captured after his frightened horse ran uncontrollably into the Union lines. Captain Howard's wounded horse also bolted from the scene and, running "at Gilpin speed," did not stop until reaching the Chancellor house—where, according to legend, Howard surrendered to General Hooker himself.[12]

Captain Keith Boswell, riding with Hill's group, was killed instantly as two musket balls entered his chest, one piercing the sketchbook he carried in his coat pocket. His spirited black stallion was seen galloping riderless toward the enemy with its chain halter rattling loosely from its neck. The horse was later captured by members of the 71st New York, who renamed the animal "Stonewall." Boswell's body, lying by the side of the Plank Road, would be found the next day by his tent mate Jed Hotchkiss, who would bury his close friend in a field on a nearby farm, all the while weeping for him "as for a brother."[13]

---

11 Whitaker, "Wounding of Jackson," 98; Thomas H. Sutton, "Additional Sketch. Eighteenth Regiment," in Walter Clark, ed., *Histories of Regiments from North Carolina*, vol. 2, 72-73.

12 Benjamin W. Leigh to wife, May 12, 1863; Palmer, "Another Account of It," 233; Taylor to *CV* magazine, January 13, 1904.

13 Hotchkiss, *Make Me a Map of the Valley*, 139-140; Randolph, "General Jackson's Mortal Wound," 334; Richard E. Wilbourn to Jubal A. Early, March 3, 1873; H. L. Potter, *The National Tribune*, October 18, 1888; J. S. Thompson, *The National Tribune*, February 14, 1889. Hotchkiss states the bullets that struck Boswell passed through the chest but did not penetrate the clothes on his back. He insists the bullets were smoothbore musket balls, which thereby prove that the group was shot by Confederate troops as they were returning to the lines. See Jedediah Hotchkiss to Hunter H. McGuire, October 8, 1898, Hotchkiss Collection, reel 15, LC.

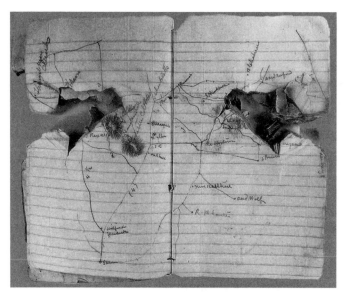

Bullet-pierced sketchbook carried in the breast pocket of
J. Keith Boswell at the time of his fatal shooting.
The Museum of the Confederacy, Richmond, Virginia

Lieutenant Taylor of Hill's staff found himself pinned to the ground after his horse was killed and then fell on top of him. General A. P. Hill had managed to leap from his horse at the start of the firing and escaped the hail of bullets by lying face down on the ground. When the shooting finally stopped, he jumped up and called out for his staff. Taylor was the only one who answered. As Hill rushed to help extricate the aide from under his horse, he shouted at the 18th North Carolina, "You have shot your friends, you have destroyed my staff!" He was still in the process of assisting Taylor when a courier ran up and informed him that Jackson had been wounded. "Help yourself," Hill told Taylor, "I must go to General Jackson."[14]

The unexpected volley that decimated Hill's group had also exacted a toll on Jackson's escort. Thrown from his horse as the animal fell dead from a gunshot, Joseph Morrison crashed into a tree and was momentarily dazed. Coming to his senses, he leaped up and ran toward the line, shouting, "Cease firing! You are firing into our own men!" Major John D. Barry of the 18th North Carolina, believing it a trick, yelled back, "Who gave that order? It's a lie! Pour it into them, boys!" The shooting killed Sergeant Cunliffe and

14 Taylor to *CV* magazine, January 13, 1904.

wounded the courier, Johns. Smith's horse was killed, while Randolph's mount was wounded several times. Wilbourn, Wynn, and Kyle, along with their horses, escaped unharmed.

Overall, Jackson's group fared better in the firing than Hill's due to its increased distance from the line and greater shielding by the density of the woods. The Confederate army did, however, suffer the one casualty it could least afford—Stonewall Jackson.[15]

Moments before the ill-fated cry of "Yankee cavalry," Jackson had been leading his staff through the woods on a diagonal angle toward the more isolated Mountain Road. Using his left as his bridle hand, Jackson had his right hand extended in order to fend branches off his face as he rode through the tangled brush. He was within 40 yards of the 18th North Carolina when the regiment unleashed its fatal volley.

Two bullets simultaneously passed through his left arm as another .69 caliber ball entered his right palm, the latter fracturing two bones and remaining lodged within the hand. The left arm dropped limply to his side as the usually calm Little Sorrel reared away from the muzzle flash and began bounding through the woods. The horse ran under a large, overhanging pine bough that struck Jackson with such force that it knocked off his hat, lacerated his face, and nearly thrust him backward out of the saddle. Reaching the Mountain Road, Little Sorrel ran east toward the Union lines for approximately 50 yards before Jackson somehow righted himself, gripped the reins with his broken right hand, and pulled back. He managed to turn the horse around and was headed back toward his own lines as help arrived.

Having seen Jackson's horse dash through the woods, Captain Wilbourn and Private Wynn immediately rode after him, Wilbourn losing his own hat as he passed beneath the same overhanging limb. The two riders caught up with the general as he was returning toward the Confederate line, at a point on the road that was nearly opposite where he had been wounded. With Wynn riding up on Jackson's right and Wilbourn on the left, they grabbed Little Sorrel's reins, as the animal was still "almost frantic from fright."

---

15 Joseph G. Morrison to Spier Whitaker, June 27, 1900; Morrison, "Stonewall Jackson at Chancellorsville," 230; [Joseph G. Morrison], "Wounding of Lieutenant-General T. J. Jackson," in *The Land We Love* (July 1866), 182. The author of *The Land We Love* account is anonymous, but in his *CV* article of 1905, Joseph Morrison admitted to being the writer.

An 1864 sketch by William Washington of Jackson being removed from the field.
The artist never completed the intended painting.
Print Collection, Miriam and Ira D. Wallach Division of Art, Prints, and Photographs,
The New York Public Library, Astor, Lenox and Tilden Foundations

Jackson, meanwhile, had an astonished look on his face as he stared quietly down the road in the direction of his line.

Looking around, the two signal men noticed the presence of an unfamiliar solitary rider standing nearby. Pointing toward the Confederate line, Wynn directed the soldier to go back and "see what troops those are." Without saying a word, the mysterious rider trotted off in the direction of the Rebel lines.[16]

16 Richard E. Wilbourn to Charles Faulkner, May 1863; Richard E. Wilbourn to Robert Dabney, December 12, 1863; Richard E. Wilbourn to Jubal A. Early, March 3, 1873. In his book *Stonewall Jackson: A Military Biography*, John Esten Cooke dramatized the presence of the solitary rider, calling it a "singular circumstance" and commenting, "Who this silent personage was is left to conjecture" (p. 422). Joseph W. Revere, a former Union general, claimed to be the individual in his book *Keel and Saddle, a Retrospect of Forty Years of Military and Naval Service* (Boston, MA, 1872), 277. His claim was completely discounted

"They certainly must be our troops," Wilbourn said to Jackson, who silently nodded his head in agreement. "General, are you hurt much?" the signal officer inquired.

"I fear my arm is broken," Jackson replied.

"Where are you struck?" Wilbourn asked, while glancing at the general's sleeves. Jackson estimated his wound to be "about half-way between the elbow and shoulder."

"Try to work your fingers," Wilbourn suggested. "If you can move your fingers at all, the arm is not broken."

Looking down at his left hand, Jackson tried to move the digits. "Yes, it is broken," he remarked. "I can't work my fingers."[17]

Growing more concerned, Wilbourn then asked whether he was hurt anywhere else.

"Yes," he answered, "[a] slight wound in the right hand." Commenting further that his left arm was "very painful," Jackson requested that the young officer see how much it was bleeding. When Wilbourn gently grasped the arm he could feel warm blood flowing down the sleeve of the india rubber raincoat Jackson was wearing. Noticing the general was becoming perceptibly weaker, he said, "I will have to rip your sleeve to get at your wound."

"Well you had better take me down too," Jackson replied. Realizing the general was too weak to ride back to the line and unsure whether they would be fired upon again as they approached, Wilbourn quickly decided the best course of action was to get Jackson down and out of sight of the troops. He dismounted as the wounded general began leaning to the left and toward him.

"Hold on, Captain," Jackson said. "You had better take me on the other side."

---

by Jubal A. Early in his article, "Stonewall Jackson—The Story of His Being an Astrologer Refuted—An Eyewitness Describes How He Was Wounded," in *SHSP* (1878), vol. 6, 261-282. Douglas Southall Freeman speculates the rider was courier David Kyle, in *Lee's Lieutenants*, vol. 2, 569. Wilbourn maintained it was an insignificant event and that Cooke made it "appear more like a romance than reality." See Richard E. Wilbourn to Jubal A. Early, February 19, 1873, Jubal Anderson Early Papers, vol. 6. LC.

17 Richard E. Wilbourn to Charles Faulkner, May 1863; Richard E. Wilbourn to Robert Dabney, December 12, 1863.

Engraving of the wounded Jackson after being removed from his horse.
Print Collection, Miriam and Ira D. Wallach Division of Art, Prints, and Photographs,
The New York Public Library, Astor, Lenox and Tilden Foundations

As Wilbourn straightened Jackson in the saddle, the general suddenly became faint. "No, go ahead," he said, before collapsing back into the arms of his signal officer. Jackson's feet were still in the stirrups, so Wynn quickly removed the general's right foot before running to the other side of Little

Sorrel to remove the left. With Wilbourn holding Jackson's upper body and Wynn his legs, the two men carried the general through the woods toward the main road. They stopped in the brush along the edge of the Plank Road and laid Jackson on the ground under a small tree. Using his thighs as a pillow, Wilbourn softly leaned the general's head into his lap and ordered Wynn to first find an ambulance and then Maj. Hunter H. McGuire, the corps medical director. He cautioned the private to keep secret from the troops the fact that Jackson had been wounded.

For the moment, Wilbourn and Jackson were alone. Not sure whether the general was still conscious, the young officer spoke up. "General, it is most remarkable that any of us escaped."

"Yes," Jackson replied. "It is providential."[18]

---

18 Richard E. Wilbourn to Charles Faulkner, May 1863; Richard E. Wilbourn to Robert Dabney, December 12, 1863.

Chapter Six

Don't Trouble Yourself About Me

Captain Richard Wilbourn was experiencing the "saddest hour of my life" as he knelt in a gloomy Wilderness thicket with a possibly dying Stonewall Jackson in front of him. With only a small penknife, the young Mississippian carefully began cutting open the left sleeve of the general's raincoat. Finding Jackson's accoutrements in the way, Wilbourn removed the "field glasses and his haversack—containing some paper, envelopes, and two religious tracts . . . and put them on myself in order to preserve them."

"Captain," Jackson said as Wilbourn continued cutting the sleeve, "I wish you would get me a skillful surgeon."

"I have sent for Doctor McGuire and also an ambulance," Wilbourn assured him. "But as Doctor McGuire may be some distance off, I will get the nearest surgeon to be found, in case you need immediate attention."[1]

Through the moonlight, Wilbourn recognized the silhouette of A. P. Hill and a few of his regrouped staff riding down the road, and called out to Hill.

---

1 Richard E. Wilbourn to Charles Faulkner, May 1863; Richard E. Wilbourn to Robert Dabney, December 12, 1863.

Jackson's haversack and binoculars.
The Museum of the Confederacy, Richmond, Virginia
Photography by Katherine Wetzel

The general, along with his aide Benjamin Leigh and signal officer Capt. Richard H. Adams, dismounted and walked over. After informing them that Jackson was wounded, Wilbourn asked Hill whether he had a surgeon with him.

"No," Hill replied, "[b]ut I can get you one." He instructed Leigh to find Brig. Gen. Dorsey Pender's brigade, which was advancing up the Plank Road, and bring its surgeon. "General," Hill said as he knelt down beside Jackson, "I am sorry to see you wounded and hope you are not badly hurt."

"My arm is broken," Jackson replied.

"Is it very painful?" Hill asked.

"Very painful," Jackson responded.[2]

---

2   Richard E. Wilbourn to Charles Faulkner, May 1863; Richard E. Wilbourn to Robert Dabney, December 12, 1863; Benjamin W. Leigh to wife, May 12, 1863.

After learning that Jackson was also wounded in the right hand, Hill removed both of the general's blood-filled gloves. Switching positions with Wilbourn, Hill then supported Jackson's back and held the left elbow while the signal officer resumed cutting away the sleeve. Underneath the raincoat, Jackson was wearing his new wool dress coat and two shirts. Wilbourn remarked that he would have to cut away all of the sleeves to get at the wound.

"That is right," Jackson said. "Cut away everything."[3]

Once the arm was exposed, it became evident that a ball had passed through the extremity just beneath the shoulder. The area was very swollen but, fortunately, the increased pressure from the swelling had helped control the hemorrhage, so bleeding from the wound was now slight. Taking a handkerchief, Wilbourn tied it around the arm just above the wound, and used another one to fashion a sling. No one at the moment, including Jackson, realized that the entrance and exit wounds from a third ball existed in the general's left forearm. After binding the arm, Wilbourn asked what he should do with the right hand.

"Don't mind that," Jackson said. "It is of little consequence and not very painful."[4]

Meanwhile, Leigh had ridden back approximately 100 yards, where he met Pender leading his brigade up the road. He told the general of Jackson's wounding and that he had been sent back to locate a surgeon. Pender immediately called for Assistant Surgeon Richard R. Barr of the 34th North Carolina, who "speedily appeared." Barr informed Leigh there was no ambulance within a mile of the position, but he did have a litter team traveling with him. They were just about to head to the scene when Jackson's

---

3 Jackson's blood-stained gloves with a bullet hole in the right palm and another at the top of the left glove were found on the battlefield by a soldier, who had them sent to Anna Jackson. See William D. Covington to Anna Jackson, June 26, 1863, Roy Bird Cook Collection, West Virginia University, and *The Sentinel* (Richmond, VA), June 27, 1863. The air temperature at the time of the wounding was likely warm. The recorded temperature 60 miles north in Washington, D.C., at 9:00 pm was 63°F. See "Record of Events Database, Valley of the Shadow: Two Communities in the American Civil War," *Virginia Center for Digital History*, University of Virginia. The fact that Jackson was wearing four layers of clothing in such warm weather could be related to the illness he had contracted the night before his wounding.

4 Richard E. Wilbourn to Charles Faulkner, May 1863; Richard E. Wilbourn to Robert Dabney, December 12, 1863.

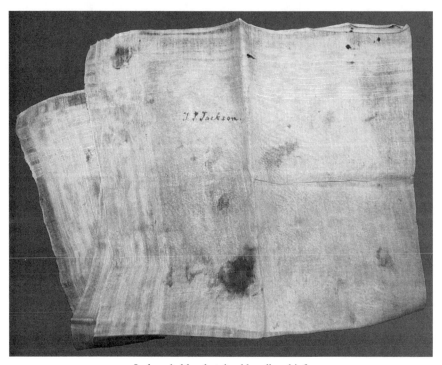

Jackson's blood-stained handkerchief.
VMI Museum, Lexington, Virginia

aide-de-camp, Lt. James Smith, who had been directing communications farther to the rear, rode up and asked Leigh for Jackson's whereabouts. Smith had been riding to the front earlier when he encountered Murray Taylor of Hill's staff, who had informed him that Jackson was wounded. Smith, Leigh, and Barr rushed back to the thicket, leaving orders for the litter team to follow.[5]

Arriving at the scene, Barr immediately examined Jackson's wound. Although he had a tourniquet with him, the surgeon decided not to use it, as the bleeding was sufficiently under control. After Barr left to obtain more supplies, Jackson looked at Hill and whispered, "Is that man a skillful surgeon?"

"I don't know much about him," Hill stated. "But he stands very high with his brigade." Realizing the concern behind Jackson's question, he

---

5 Benjamin W. Leigh to wife, May 12, 1863.

quickly added, "He does not propose to do anything and is here only in readiness, in case anything should be required before Dr. McGuire arrives."

"Very good," replied Jackson, satisfied. Joseph Morrison now arrived and, falling to the ground beside his brother-in-law, "expressed great sympathy" at his being wounded.[6]

Captain Adams, who was carrying a canteen of water and a captured flask of whiskey, offered Jackson a drink of alcohol as a stimulant. Jackson refused at first, but after Wilbourn insisted it would help revive him, the general asked whether it could be mixed with water. Hill encouraged Jackson to drink the whiskey straight first and then follow it with water, which he did for several swallows. After Jackson finished, Wilbourn offered to pour some of the water canteen's remaining contents over his wound.

"Yes, if you please," the general said. "Pour it so as to wet the cloth." Jackson was a firm believer in hydropathy. The so-called "water cure," developed by Vincenz Priessnitz in Austria in the 1820s, used cold water as a treatment for a variety of medical problems. Jackson had been introduced to the therapy in 1851 through an acquaintance whose father was a physician practicing hydropathy.[7]

Suddenly, two Yankee soldiers, rifles in hand, emerged from the bushes fewer than 20 feet away. Seeing them, Hill ordered, "Take charge of those men." Adams and a courier instantly called for them to surrender. The startled men dropped their muskets, commenting, "We were not aware that we were in your lines."[8]

6   Richard E. Wilbourn to Charles Faulkner, May 1863; Richard E. Wilbourn to Robert Dabney, December 12, 1863; James P. Smith to Jedediah Hotchkiss, (n.d.), Miscellaneous Manuscripts, New York Historical Society (NYHS). Benjamin Wright, surgeon with the 55th Virginia, wrote an account stating that Hill brought him to the area and he was the first physician to examine Jackson. Wright, however, is not mentioned in any of the first-person accounts. See Benjamin P. Wright, "Recollections of the Battle of Chancellorsville and the Wounding of General Jackson," bound volume 176, FSNMP.

7   Richard E. Wilbourn to Charles Faulkner, May 1863; Richard E. Wilbourn to Robert Dabney, December 12, 1863; Richard E. Wilbourn to Jubal A. Early, February 19, 1873; Murray F. Taylor to the *CV*, January 13, 1904; "Stonewall Jackson and the Henderson Hydropath," *Samaritan Health Newsletter* (September 2008), issue 42.

8   Joseph G. Morrison to Robert Dabney, October 29, 1863, Charles William Dabney Papers, SHC, University of North Carolina; Richard E. Wilbourn to Charles Faulkner, May 1863; Richard E. Wilbourn to Robert Dabney, December 12, 1863.

Concerned this was an indication the enemy was advancing, Morrison stepped out onto the Plank Road and walked east for 20 yards before the sight of the enemy caused him to freeze in his tracks. Through the moonlight, he could see the outline of Union cannon unlimbering in the road fewer than 100 yards away. He returned to the group and anxiously related that the Yankees were nearby and closing.

With Jackson injured, Hill, his senior divisional commander, needed to leave and assume command of the corps. He rose to his feet and told Jackson that he would try to keep the wounding a secret from the troops. Leaving Leigh to assist with Jackson's care, Hill and the rest of his staff mounted their horses and galloped back up the road.

Those in the group around Jackson were now in a precarious situation. They remained between the lines and, before long, fighting was sure to resume in the area. Instead of continuing to wait for an ambulance, they decided it would be best to get Jackson away from the area to prevent his possible capture. Morrison suggested they pick the general up in their arms and carry him off.

"No," Jackson offered, "If you will help me up, I can walk."[9]

Leaning on Leigh's left shoulder, Jackson unsteadily made his way through the bushes and onto the Plank Road, rapidly filling with Confederate troops rushing forward to meet the Union advance. Although Jackson was undoubtedly in pain, Leigh related later that he was "calm and did not utter a groan."

To conceal the general from the men rushing forward, they walked along the edge of the road, with Wilbourn screening the group by leading horses between them and the open road. Despite their best efforts, passing men could still see a wounded man, surrounded by officers, being led from the field. Several curious soldiers inquired as to the identity of the wounded person, and each time he was questioned Wilbourn responded that it was only a wounded friend. "When asked, just say it is a Confederate officer," Jackson instructed him after repeated inquiries.

Unsatisfied by this evasive response, Sgt. Tom Fogg of the 55th Virginia maneuvered around the horses to get a better look. "Great God!" he

---

9   Joseph G. Morrison to Robert Dabney, October 29, 1863; Richard E. Wilbourn to Charles Faulkner, May 1863; Richard E. Wilbourn to Robert Dabney, December 12, 1863; Richard E. Wilbourn to Jubal A. Early, February 19, 1873.

Remains of the stretcher believed
to be the one used to remove
Jackson from the field.
Gettysburg National Military Park

exclaimed. "That is General Jackson!" Wilbourn told Fogg he was mistaken, it was simply a Confederate officer. With a puzzled look on his face, the sergeant walked off without saying another word.[10]

After traveling a short distance on the road, the group finally met Barr's litter team and stopped momentarily to lay Jackson on the canvas stretcher. With Smith and one litter bearer at the front two corners and Morrison and another bearer at the back two, the men lifted the stretcher to their shoulders and began moving rapidly toward the rear. They had preceded only a few steps when the Union battery Morrison had seen on the Plank Road suddenly opened fire, raking the pathway with what Wilbourn described as "terrific fire of grape, shell, and canister."

The horses Wilbourn was leading jerked loose and ran

10 Benjamin W. Leigh to wife, May 12, 1863; Richard E. Wilbourn to Charles Faulkner, May 1863; Richard E. Wilbourn to Robert Dabney, December 12, 1863; Richard E. Wilbourn to Jubal A. Early, February 19, 1873; Albert Rennolds, "Virginia Reminiscences," in *CV* (February 1897), 51-52.

wild. Soldiers rushing to the front dove to the ground or jumped into the woods to escape the barrage. "Riderless and panic stricken horses were running here and there," Wilbourn observed, "and missiles of every caliber and description were falling in every direction, and for a while, everything seemed to be in confusion."[11]

A piece of shrapnel tore into the right shoulder of Pvt. John J. Johnson of the 22nd Virginia, the litter bearer carrying the front corner across from Jimmy Smith. The injury caused Johnson to drop the stretcher from his left shoulder, but a quick-acting Leigh caught the handle before the litter could tilt enough to roll Jackson off. After hurriedly lowering the stretcher to the ground, the other litter bearer ran for cover in the woods, leaving Smith, Morrison, and Leigh to throw their bodies next to Jackson's to shield him from the cannon fire.[12]

Lying on the ground beside Jackson, the three courageous officers watched sparks fly from the road as shrapnel ricocheted off small rocks around them. Smith thought his own life was going to end there, writing later: "It was my solemn expectation to die by the side of him whose side I had been proud to ride on day of battle." Realizing the situation, Jackson attempted to rise so all could move to the shelter of the woods. "It will cost you your life sir, if you get up," Smith shouted as he pulled Jackson back down. "Wait a minute."[13]

After sending a barrage of more than a dozen rounds down the road, the Union battery elevated its guns and resumed firing. With the shells now sailing slightly overhead, the road became less hazardous, and Jackson rose to his feet. Leaning on Smith for support, he walked into the thicket, with Leigh behind him carrying the litter. Making their way through woods that Morrison said were "filled with whistling canister and shrieking shell," the group encountered Gen. Dorsey Pender. "General, I am sorry to see you

---

11 Richard E. Wilbourn to Robert Dabney, December 12, 1863.

12 Richard E. Wilbourn to Charles Faulkner, May 1863; Benjamin W. Leigh to wife, May 12, 1863; James P. Smith to Jedediah Hotchkiss, n.d.; James P. Smith, "Lt. Smith Narrative," Dabney-Jackson Collection, box 2, LVA. Since the event, there has been debate as to whether Jackson fell off the litter when Johnson was wounded. See Appendix I for a discussion of the topic.

13 [Morrison], "Wounding of Lieutenant-General T. J. Jackson," 182; Smith to Hotchkiss, n.d.; Smith, "Lt. Smith Narrative."

have been wounded," Pender said to Jackson. "The lines are so much broken that I fear we will have to fall back."

"You must hold your ground, General Pender," Jackson ordered in a weak but authoritative tone. "You must hold your ground, sir."[14]

The arduous walk through the woods began to take a toll on Jackson; he soon became fatigued and lightheaded. After placing him back on the stretcher, Leigh tried to solicit nearby soldiers to help in bearing the litter. None were willing to do so for a "Confederate officer," so Leigh had to tell them it was Jackson who was wounded. In an instant, men sprang forward to help. Lifting the stretcher to their shoulders, four soldiers carried the litter with great difficulty through the thick undergrowth of the Wilderness.

Then, "[a]s we were going through the woods," Leigh wrote, "one of the litter bearers got his foot tangled in a grapevine and fell," dropping his corner of the litter. With no one close enough to catch the handle this time, the stretcher tilted and Jackson rolled off, falling several feet before landing hard on his wounded arm. For the first time, he let out an expression of pain and exhaustion. "He must have suffered excruciating agonies," Leigh commented. More troubling, the sharp edge of a broken bone damaged the brachial artery in the upper arm and fresh blood flowed from the wound.[15]

Kneeling on the ground, Smith gently lifted the general's head. In the filtered moonlight, he could see that Jackson's eyes were closed and his face pale. Fearful he was "breathing his life away," Smith said to him, "General, are you hurt much?"

"No, my friend," Jackson replied, opening his eyes. "Don't trouble yourself about me."[16]

Placing Jackson back on the litter, the group continued its journey to the rear, this time back along the road in order to avoid a repeat mishap of someone tripping in the brush. Growing weaker as he lost blood, Jackson asked for more alcohol as a stimulant. As none of those present had any

14 [Morrison], "Wounding of Lieutenant-General T. J. Jackson," 182; Smith to Hotchkiss, n.d.; Smith, "Lt. Smith Narrative."

15 Benjamin W. Leigh to wife, May 12, 1863; Richard E. Wilbourn to Charles Faulkner, May 1863. A brief item in the *Southern Historical Society Papers* claims a soldier named D. W. Busick was the litter bearer who tripped, not on a vine but on the leg of another soldier. See *SHSP* (1882), vol. 10, 143.

16 Smith to Hotchkiss, n.d.; Smith, "Lt. Smith Narrative."

Shell jacket worn by James P. Smith during Jackson's removal from the field.
Blood stains on the front are from Jackson.
The Museum of the Confederacy, Richmond, Virginia
Photography by Katherine Wetzel

whiskey, Wilbourn galloped off toward the nearest field hospital, hoping to find some medicinal spirits.

*   *   *

To the west near the old schoolhouse, Surgeon William R. Whitehead of the 44th Virginia was assisting wounded men when one of Jackson's staff recognized him. Informing Whitehead that the general was wounded, he asked the surgeon whether he could procure an ambulance and have it brought forward along the road. Whitehead immediately rode west to an open field where he had previously seen an ambulance stationed. Finding the driver, Pvt. Thomas J. Capps of the 3rd North Carolina, Whitehead asked him to take the ambulance down the Plank Road to remove a wounded officer. Capps refused to budge, saying he had explicit orders from his own regimental surgeon to remain where he was until he received further instructions. Whitehead then disclosed that the wounded officer was General Jackson. "That's enough," Capps responded, "I'll go, sir."[17]

Capps drove his two-horse team down the Plank Road through air that was "filled with shells and small shot" until he came upon a group of men crouching beside the road. "They were evidently on the look for an ambulance," Capps remembered, "and raised up and motioned to me when I drew near." But instead of finding Jackson's group, Capps had been stopped by artillery captain Marcellus Moorman as he was helping Col. Stapleton Crutchfield, Jackson's chief of artillery, who had been wounded in the left thigh. Also present was Maj. Arthur L. Rogers, an artillery officer wounded in the arm. They had just finished placing Crutchfield in the ambulance and Rogers was climbing in when Jimmy Smith ran up the road shouting for them to wait.[18]

Spotting the ambulance in the road, Smith had run ahead of the litter team in order to secure the use of the wagon. The standard four-wheeled ambulance in use at the time had a spring-loaded suspension and a canvas cover stretched over a wood frame. As the wagon could carry only two recumbent men comfortably, Major Rogers agreed to forgo its use to accommodate Jackson. Within moments, the litter bearers arrived with the wounded general. Dr. Whitehead, who had followed the ambulance forward, quickly felt Jackson's pulse and asked for spirits; again none were available. Jackson was placed in the ambulance next to Crutchfield, with Morrison jumping in the back between the two men and Leigh climbing on next to the driver. With Smith and Whitehead traveling alongside, the ambulance set out for the hospital. A bullet passed through the wagon's canvas top as it raced to the rear.[19]

17 William R. Whitehead, "Adventures of an American Surgeon" (1902), Denver Medical Library, Denver, Colorado; Andrew J. Howell, "The Ambulance Driver who Carried Stonewall Jackson Off the Field," Thomas J. Jackson Collection, MOC.

18 Howell, "Ambulance Driver"; Donald B. Koonce, ed., *Doctor to the Front: The Recollections of Confederate Surgeon Thomas Fanning Wood* (Knoxville, TN, 2000), 78; Moorman, "Narrative of Events," 114-115; Smith, "Lt. Smith Narrative."

19 Smith, "Lt. Smith Narrative"; Whitehead, "Adventures of an American Surgeon"; Howell, "Ambulance Driver."

Sketches of the type of stretcher and ambulance commonly used by the Confederate Army.
A Manual of Military Surgery for the Use of Surgeons in the
Confederate States Army with Explanatory Plates of all Useful Operations

The Melzi Chancellor homestead, also known as Dowdall's Tavern, was being used as a field hospital. It contained both Union and Confederate soldiers who had been wounded during the day's battle. Capps brought the ambulance to a halt in front of the tavern while Whitehead went in to obtain spirits and water for Jackson and Crutchfield.

Farther up the road near another hospital, Maj. Hunter H. McGuire was talking to Sandie Pendleton when a courier was heard shouting, "Does anyone know where Doctor McGuire is?" After McGuire called the man over, the soldier informed him and Pendleton that Jackson had been wounded and the doctor's presence was urgently needed. They were just about to head forward when Wilbourn rode up and provided the two with further details of the tragic event. Overcome by the news, Pendleton fainted. After ensuring that the young adjutant was unharmed, McGuire and Wilbourn quickly rode east to find Jackson.[20]

The two arrived at Dowdall's Tavern shortly after the ambulance. Climbing into the back of the wagon, McGuire addressed Jackson: "I hope you are not much hurt, General."

"I am badly injured Doctor," he responded. "I fear I am dying."[21]

---

20 Hunter H. McGuire to Jubal A. Early, March 2, 1873, Jubal Anderson Early Papers, vol. 6. LC; Hunter H. McGuire, "Last Hours of Stonewall Jackson," Miscellaneous Manuscripts, NYHS; Richard E. Wilbourn to Jubal A. Early, February 19, 1873. In the "Last Hours of Stonewall Jackson," McGuire states that the name of the courier who found him was "Sherrer." In the letter to his wife, Leigh also mentions a courier named "Shearer" as being present at Dowdall's Tavern. The exact identity of this soldier, however, is unknown.

21 McGuire, "Last Hours of Stonewall Jackson."

Chapter Seven

I Thought You Were Killed

Hunter Holmes McGuire was the 27-year-old medical director of Stonewall Jackson's Second Corps. Born in Winchester, Virginia, the tall, slender McGuire sported a black mustache and was known to be an accomplished surgeon. With medical degrees from the Winchester College of Medicine and the Medical College of Virginia, McGuire was first commissioned as a surgeon in the Provisional Army of the Confederate States of America in May 1861 and was ordered to report to Harper's Ferry, Virginia (now West Virginia), as medical director of the Army of the Shenandoah. The unit was under the command of then-Col. Thomas J. Jackson.

McGuire reported for duty to Jackson after he arrived at Harper's Ferry and the two men had a brief conversation, which McGuire described as "pleasant." Jackson then directed the physician to return to quarters and await further orders. It took a week for Jackson to officially announce at a dress parade that McGuire had been appointed medical director of the army. Months later, after the two had developed a close friendship, McGuire inquired about the reason for the initial delay. "You looked so young,"

Jackson answered, "I sent to Richmond to see if there wasn't some mistake."[1]

Jackson developed complete confidence in McGuire's medical skills, beginning at the first battle of Manassas. During the engagement that inspired his famous nickname, Jackson also took a bullet in the base of his middle finger when he raised his arm in the air during the fight. "The ball," McGuire described, "struck the finger a little to one side, broke it, and carried off a small piece of the bone." Undeterred, Jackson wrapped a handkerchief around the finger and continued leading his troops until the battle was over. He then rode to the nearest field hospital, where a surgeon quickly decided that amputating the finger was necessary. But as the doctor left to prepare for surgery, Jackson quietly got back on his horse and trotted off to find McGuire.[2]

The young surgeon was busy treating the wounded at a nearby hospital when he noticed Jackson approaching. Noting the bandaged hand, McGuire walked over and asked the general whether he was seriously injured. "No," Jackson answered, "not half as badly as many here, and I will wait." He then walked over to a nearby stream, sat on the bank, and refused assistance until "his turn came." Only after McGuire had completed his immediate tasks could he persuade Jackson to allow him to examine the hand. As the surgeon looked at the finger, Jackson asked whether the injury would require an amputation. "General," McGuire replied, "if it was mine, I would try to save it."[3]

After dressing the wound with a lint bandage, McGuire placed a splint on the finger to immobilize the fracture and instructed Jackson to keep the dressing wet with cold water—a treatment embraced by the hydropathy-loving general. McGuire later observed Jackson frequently "occupied for several hours pouring cup after cup of water over his hand with the patience and perseverance for which he was so remarkable." The

1 "Sketch of the Life of Hunter Holmes McGuire," Hotchkiss Collection, reel 39, LC; Hunter H. McGuire, "Dr. McGuire Narrative," Dabney-Jackson Collection, box 2, LVA; McGuire, "Reminiscences of the Famous Leader," 301.

2 McGuire, "Reminiscences of the Famous Leader," 303-304; McGuire, "Dr. McGuire Narrative"; Jackson, *Life and Letters*, 177-178.

3 McGuire, "Reminiscences of the Famous Leader," 303-304; McGuire, "Dr. McGuire Narrative."

wound healed without complications, and "in the end, the deformity was very trifling."[4]

As McGuire approached a wounded Jackson at the battle of Chancellorsville two years later, the situation was far more serious.

"I am glad you have come," Jackson said to McGuire as he began examining the arm. "I think the wound in my shoulder is still bleeding."

Jackson's clothes were already saturated with blood and McGuire could see more oozing from the wound. Quickly placing his finger above the bullet hole, the young surgeon compressed the artery in the arm to stop the hemorrhage; otherwise, he recounted later, Jackson "would probably have died in ten minutes." Candles brought out from the tavern provided McGuire with enough light to readjust the handkerchief to help control the bleeding. Surgeon John A. Straith, in charge of the field hospital, also provided some whiskey and morphine which McGuire gave to both Jackson and Crutchfield.

Despite these efforts, Jackson's condition remained critical. "His extremities were cool, his skin clammy, his face pale, and his lips compressed and bloodless," McGuire wrote. Jackson, however, was calm and "controlled by his iron will all evidence of emotion."[5]

McGuire instructed Smith to ride forward to the larger corps hospital three miles away and have Dr. Harvey Black prepare a tent for Jackson's arrival. Ordering Capps to proceed to the hospital, McGuire sat near the front of the ambulance with his finger resting over the artery in Jackson's upper arm in the event the bleeding should restart. Leigh and others rode ahead of the wagon with torches to light the way and clear the road.[6]

After traveling a quarter of a mile, the ambulance passed Wilderness Church and arrived at the fork where the Old Turnpike and Orange Plank roads diverged on their way to the town of Orange Court House. Keeping to the right, Capps proceeded along the Old Turnpike en route to the Second Corps field hospital located at Wilderness Tavern.

It was a rough-and-tumble journey over the Old Turnpike, rutted and pitted by troop movements and fighting. At one point the ambulance had to

---

4   McGuire, "Reminiscences of the Famous Leader," 303-304.

5   McGuire, "Last Hours of Stonewall Jackson"; Smith, "Lt. Smith Narrative."

6   Smith, "Lt. Smith Narrative"; McGuire, "Last Hours of Stonewall Jackson"; Benjamin W. Leigh to wife, May 12, 1863.

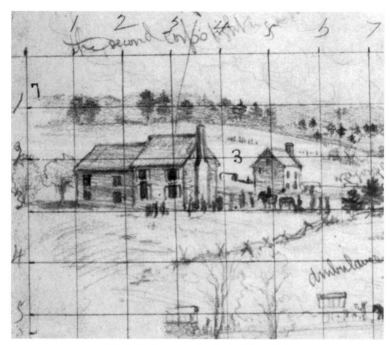

Edwin Forbes sketch of a field hospital
at Wilderness Tavern.
Library of Congress

cross a stream where the small bridge over it had been burned. The wagon lurched and jolted as it went across the rocky bed, shooting pain through the broken bones of both wounded patients. "Driver," Jackson called out, "[d]rive carefully, please."

"General, I'll do my best," Capps replied, "but if I hold in my horses, they'll be sure to balk."[7]

Along the way Jackson became more concerned about Crutchfield's condition than his own. Reaching up with his broken right hand, Jackson pulled McGuire down and quietly asked whether his artillery chief was dangerously wounded. No, the surgeon informed him, only "painfully hurt."

"Thank you," Jackson whispered, "I'm glad it is no worse."

A short distance later, Crutchfield mirrored the action, asking the same about Jackson. McGuire told him the general was "very seriously wounded."

---

7 Howell, "Ambulance Driver."

"Oh, my God!" Crutchfield cried out in response. Misinterpreting the colonel's exclamation as a cry of pain, Jackson promptly ordered McGuire to stop the ambulance and see about relieving the officer's discomfort.[8]

* * *

Wilderness Tavern was actually a collection of structures along the Old Turnpike consisting of the tavern, a house, shops, and stables. A sprawling Confederate corps hospital had been established at the site using the buildings and a network of tents stretching across open fields on both sides of the road. The complex was under the immediate direction of Dr. Harvey Black, a native of Blacksburg, Virginia (his family had founded the town in 1798), and McGuire's second in command with regard to corps medical duties. Having been informed by Smith of Jackson's impending arrival, Black had readied a large bell tent complete with a bed, warm blankets, and a stove with a fire. The tent sat in a field on the north side of the Old Turnpike a little more than 100 yards from the main structures at Wilderness Tavern.[9]

It was close to 11:30 p.m. when the ambulance finally arrived at the hospital. An exhausted Jackson was carried into the warm tent and gently laid in bed. He had lost a great deal of blood and his diminished pulse indicated to McGuire that he was too weak to tolerate surgery. The only means available to treat shock in 1863 were to keep the patient warm and still, so the surgeons gave Jackson another drink of whiskey, covered him with blankets, and instructed him to rest. McGuire would know over the next few hours whether or not Jackson would recover. The general fell into a deep sleep while the group kept a close vigil at his bedside.

The medical staff tried to suppress knowledge of Jackson's condition, but word spread through the camp as the night progressed. "For some time after he was brought in, his being wounded was kept from the soldiers as much as possible," recalled John S. Apperson, a hospital steward. "I noticed

---

8 Hunter H. McGuire, "Death of Stonewall Jackson," in *SHSP* (1886), vol. 14, 156; McGuire, "Last Hours of Stonewall Jackson."

9 Black started the war as regimental surgeon of the 4th Virginia. In December 1862, he was appointed by McGuire to be the surgeon in charge of the newly created field hospital of the Second Corps. Despite his direct involvement in Jackson's surgery and care, Black does not mention the event in his surviving letters. See Glenn L. McMullen, ed., *A Surgeon with Stonewall Jackson: The Civil War Letters of Dr. Harvey Black* (Baltimore, MD, 1995).

Drs. Black and McGuire were in close conversation and the subject was of serious import I could well see. Sometime during the night Dr. Black told us that Gen. Jackson had been wounded. How seriously he did not say."[10]

Jackson's pulse steadily improved, and two and a half hours after his arrival at the hospital it had become significantly stronger. The surgeons concluded that he was stable enough to undergo a more thorough examination of the wounds, followed by possible amputation of the arm. Timing was important. Much like the "golden hour" concept in trauma care today, Civil War surgeons had found that when surgery was necessary, the sooner it occurred after injury, the better the soldier's chance of survival. The considerable tissue damage and multiple fractures that accompanied many of the gunshot wounds to extremities during the war were also better managed by amputation, as leaving the damaged fragments intact often led to a serious bone infection known as osteomyelitis.[11]

McGuire woke Jackson and informed him of the plan to administer chloroform as an anesthetic, followed by a close examination of his wounds. The entire process would be painless. If the exam revealed that amputation of the arm was needed, McGuire wanted to know whether he should proceed with the operation.

"Yes, certainly, Dr. McGuire," Jackson replied. "Do for me whatever you think best."

In addition to Black, McGuire enlisted the help of surgeons J. William Walls and Robert T. Coleman. The two most difficult parts of the operation, the administration of chloroform and the amputation itself, would be handled by Black and McGuire, respectively. Coleman would monitor the general's pulse throughout the procedure while Walls directly assisted

---

10 Ibid., 2.

11 McGuire, "Last Hours of Stonewall Jackson." *In A Manual of Military Surgery for the Use of Surgeons in the Confederate States Army* (Columbia, SC, 1864), author J. Julian Chisolm wrote: "[I]n gunshot fracture of the long bones remove, without fail, and as soon after the accident as possible, all fragments of bone" (368). Despite using unsterile techniques and lacking antibiotics, the Civil War mortality rate following amputation of the upper one-third of the arm—the surgery Jackson received—was only 13.6 percent. See George A. Otis, *Medical and Surgical History of the War of the Rebellion* (Washington, D.C., 1876), pt. 2, vol. 2, 698.

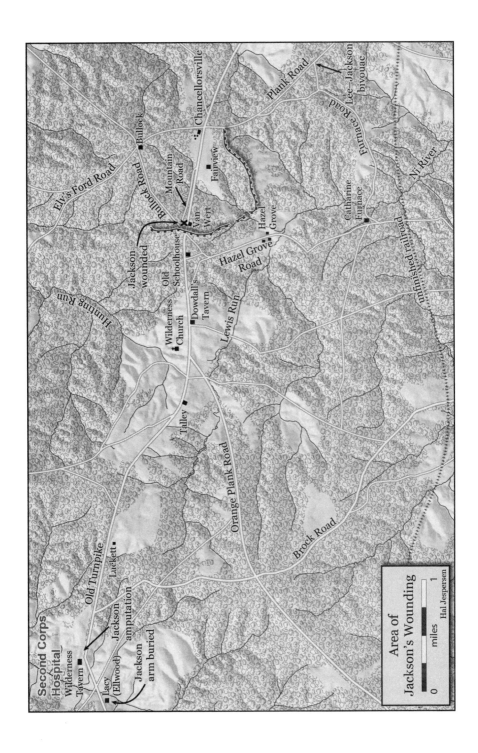

Area of
Jackson's Wounding

0   miles   1

Hal Jespersen

McGuire. The ever-present Jimmy Smith would stand nearby holding a candle for extra light.[12]

At 2:00 a.m., now May 3, 1863, Black took a cloth folded in the shape of a cone with a chloroform-soaked sponge in its point and positioned it over the general's nose and mouth. As he inhaled the sweet-smelling anesthetic, Jackson's pain began to melt away. "What an infinite blessing," he muttered. He continued to softly repeat the word "blessing" as he faded into a twilight stage of consciousness.

McGuire carefully examined Jackson's left arm, noting that a bullet had passed through the extremity about three inches below the shoulder joint, shattering the bone. The damaged brachial artery left McGuire with no other options: he would have to amputate the limb. He then noticed the other wound in the arm. A second bullet, he recorded, had "entered on the outside of the forearm an inch below the elbow joint and came out upon the inside of the forearm an inch above the wrist joint." The third bullet still lodged in Jackson's right hand had "entered the palm about the middle of the hand and had fractured two of the bones." The general had also suffered facial lacerations when his frantic horse ran under the tree limb.[13]

McGuire started the operation after the examination was complete. First, he extracted the bullet from the right hand. It was a round ball fired from a smoothbore musket, a clear indication that the shot had come from the Confederate side, as Union soldiers were no longer using the older weapons. He turned and handed the ball to Smith, who would later give it to Anna Jackson.

---

12 McGuire, "Last Hours of Stonewall Jackson"; Smith, "Lt. Smith Narrative." Dabney and subsequent authors listed Black as monitoring the pulse and Coleman giving the anesthetic, but Smith's narrative clearly states: "chloroform administered by Dr. Black, Coleman watched pulse, McGuire amputated and Walls took up arteries." Given Black's position and experience, he most likely performed the delicate job of administering the anesthetic. J. William Walls was the regimental surgeon of the 5th Virginia and was a faculty member of the Winchester Medical College prior to the Civil War. For a brief biographical sketch, see *Transactions of the Medical and Chirurgical Faculty of the State of Maryland* (Baltimore, MD, 1881), 35-36. Robert T. Coleman was the chief surgeon of Isaac Trimble's division in the Second Corps. For a brief biographical sketch, see William B. Atkinson, *A Biographical Dictionary of Contemporary American Physicians and Surgeons* (Philadelphia, PA, 1880), 286-287.

13 McGuire, "Last Hours of Stonewall Jackson"; Hunter H. McGuire, "Last Wound of the Late Gen. Jackson (Stonewall)—The Amputation of the Arm—His Last Moments and Death," *Richmond Medical Journal* (1866), vol. 1, 403-412; Smith, "Lt. Smith Narrative."

Moving to the left arm, McGuire performed a circular amputation. Taking a long, sharp surgical knife, he made an incision through the skin, muscles, and other soft tissue in a circular motion around the arm down to the bone. Surgeon Walls then tied off the artery and retracted the soft tissue toward the shoulder for several inches in order to expose an intact segment of bone. McGuire cut through the visible bone with an amputation saw. When the retracted tissue was released, it covered the end of the bone and McGuire sutured the incision to close the wound and form a stump. The entire procedure was completed within minutes and with minimal loss of blood. McGuire finished by placing a dressing over the stump and covering Jackson's facial lacerations with isinglass plaster, a precursor to modern-day adhesive bandages.[14]

With the surgery complete and Jackson resting comfortably, McGuire needed to assist with the care of other wounded soldiers at the hospital. He instructed Smith to watch the general closely and send for him immediately if there was any change. In half an hour, he would have coffee sent over and Smith was to wake Jackson and have him drink a cup.

The coffee arrived at the appropriate time and Smith was easily able to arouse the general and ask whether he would take some. Jackson drank half a pint, commenting that the coffee was "very good, refreshing." Fully awake, Jackson looked at the stump and realized he had lost his arm. "Were you here?" he asked Smith, referring to the operation. Yes, the lieutenant answered, he had been present for the entire procedure. After a moment of reflection, Jackson asked whether he had said anything while under the influence of chloroform, as it was the most pleasant physical sensation he had ever enjoyed. "I think I had enough consciousness to know what was happening," Jackson continued, "and at one time thought I heard the most delightful music that ever greeted my ears—I believe it was the sawing of the bone."[15]

*   *   *

14 McGuire would later write in letter dated March 7, 1870, that he believed the wounds in the left arm were also made by round balls fired from a smooth-bore musket. See "How Stonewall Jackson Died," *De Bow's Review* (May/June 1870), vol. 8, 477-478.

15 McGuire, "Last Hours of Stonewall Jackson"; Smith, "Lt. Smith Narrative."

Robert E. Lee was sleeping in his tent when he was awakened by voices outside. Wilbourn was there, having been sent by Pendleton to inform the commanding general of the night's events. Entering Lee's tent, the signal officer gave a detailed account of the fighting and the current position of the opposing armies.

Then Wilbourn sadly reported that Jackson had been wounded and taken to a field hospital. "Thank God it is no worse," Lee said. "God be praised that he is yet alive." After a brief reflective pause, he added, "Ah, Captain, any victory is dearly bought that deprives us of the services of Jackson even for a short time."

Wilbourn started to describe Jackson's wounds and the way he had received them when Lee stopped him: "Captain, don't let us say anything more about it. It is too painful to talk about." Hotchkiss arrived at Lee's tent about an hour later and also began to tell him of Jackson's wounding. "I know all about it and do not wish to hear any more," Lee said to him. "It is too painful a subject."[16]

Back at the corps hospital, Jackson completed two important tasks while still awake following his surgery. The first was to ask Joseph Morrison to go to Richmond and bring Anna Jackson (Morrison's sister) to be with him while he recovered. He then dictated a message to Lee informing him of his wounding and that he had turned command of the corps over to A. P. Hill. Jackson then drifted back to sleep.

He would rest only briefly before being awakened again, however. Around 3:30 a.m., Sandie Pendleton arrived and asked McGuire whether he could speak to the general. The surgeon at first refused on the grounds that Jackson needed rest. It was important, Pendleton said: the battle was turning. A. P. Hill had also been wounded, and cavalry general Jeb Stuart had been summoned to the front to assume overall command. "Mac," Pendleton implored, "the safety of his army and the success of our cause depends upon my seeing him." After a brief check on Jackson's condition, McGuire allowed Pendleton to enter.

"Well, Major," said Jackson to the adjutant as he walked into the tent, "I am glad to see you, very glad. I thought you were killed."

---

16 Richard E. Wilbourn to Charles Faulkner, May 1863; Richard E. Wilbourn to Robert Dabney, December 12, 1863; Richard E. Wilbourn to Jubal A. Early, February 19, 1873.

Pendleton reported on the current state of affairs, and said Stuart wanted to know the general's intentions. Jackson tried to concentrate his thoughts. For a moment, McGuire observed, "his nostrils dilated" and "his eyes flashed its old fire" as if he was about to enter battle, but soon his face relaxed as his weakness returned.

"I don't know. I can't tell," Jackson sighed. "[S]ay to General Stuart that he must do what he thinks best."

Pendleton walked out. With tears welling up in his eyes, he commented to McGuire, "We didn't know what he was worth, Mac, 'til we lost him."[17]

Jackson slipped back into sleep and McGuire resumed his work tending to the wounded, checking in on the general every hour and finding him asleep each time. Jim Lewis also arrived at some point during the night to help with his care, bringing food and another blanket.

Around 9:00 a.m., booming cannon from the renewed fighting around Chancellorsville again woke Jackson from his sleep. Drinking more coffee, he expressed the belief that he would fully recover from his wounds. A courier then arrived with Lee's response to Jackson's earlier message. Smith read it out loud:

General: I have just received your note, informing me you were wounded. I cannot express my regret at the occurrence. Could I have directed events, I should have chosen, for the good of the country, to have been disabled in your stead.

I congratulate you upon the victory which is due to your skill and energy.

> Most truly yours,
> R. E. Lee, General[18]

Turning his head aside after Smith finished, Jackson quietly remarked, "General Lee is very kind, but he should give the praise to God." Then looking back at Smith, he took the opportunity to quiz the young divinity

---

17 Joseph G. Morrison to Spier Whitaker, June 27, 1900; James P. Smith to Jedediah Hotchkiss, April 30, 1886, Jed Hotchkiss Papers, VHS; Smith, "Lt. Smith Narrative"; McGuire, "Last Hours of Stonewall Jackson."

18 Smith, "Stonewall Jackson's Last Battle," 213.

student. "Can you tell me where the Bible gives generals a model for their official reports of battles?" Laughing, Smith said he had never thought of looking to the scriptures for such guidance. "Nevertheless," Jackson replied, "there are such, and excellent models too. Look for instance at the narrative of Joshua's battles with the Amalekites—there you have one. It has clearness, brevity, modesty; and it traces the victory to its right source, the blessing of God."[19]

At 10:00 a.m., McGuire came in on his hourly rounds to find Jackson awake and talkative. The general had one complaint: pain in his right side. He asked the physician to take a look at the area, as he believed he had struck it against a stone or stump when he fell from the litter the night before. McGuire performed a careful examination, but could find no signs of injury: "The skin was not bruised or broken and the lung performed as far as I could tell, its proper function." The surgeon prescribed a "simple application and rub"—most likely a mustard plaster—and told Jackson the pain should diminish momentarily.[20]

Distinct sounds of cannon fire and musketry from the battle could still be heard, and Jackson insisted that McGuire leave him to supervise removing the wounded and to visit the other hospitals. McGuire reluctantly agreed, but instructed Smith to remain with the general and to send for Black if he needed anything.

Tucker Lacy now arrived and asked whether he could visit with Jackson. Entering the tent and seeing the bandaged stump, the pastor exclaimed, "Oh General, what a calamity!" Jackson quickly tried to reassure him:

> You find me severely wounded but not unhappy or depressed. I believe that it has been done according to the will of God and I acquiesce entirely in his holy will. It may appear strange, but you never saw me more perfectly contented than I am today; for I am sure that my heavenly father designs this affliction for my good. I am perfectly satisfied that either in this life or the life which is to come, I shall discover that what is now regarded as a calamity, is a blessing. And if it is regarded as a calamity (for surely I will

---

19 Henderson, *Stonewall Jackson and the American Civil War*, vol. 2, 380-381.

20 McGuire, "Last Hours of Stonewall Jackson"; McGuire, "Last Wound of the Late Gen. Jackson (Stonewall)," 407. Mustard is a rubefacient, or skin irritant, that does not cause blistering, and was used to create a reaction of warmth in the same fashion as mild irritant creams are used today.

feel it to be a great inconvenience to be deprived of my arm) it will result in a great blessing. I can wait until God, in his own time shall make known to me the object he has in thus afflicting me. But why should not I rather rejoice in it as a blessing and not look upon it as a calamity at all? If it were in my power to replace my arm and to restore myself to perfect health, I should not dare to do it, unless I had reason to believe it was the will of God.[21]

"If it be best for you," the pastor asked him, "how is it with the country?"

"It is no doubt best for the country also," he answered, "and that will, by and by, be seen."[22]

After further relating to Lacy the circumstances of the event, Jackson said of the wounding: "I thought after I fell from the litter, that I would die upon the field and I gave myself up into the hands of my heavenly father without a fear. I was in the possession of perfect peace. It has been a valuable and precious experience to me, that I was brought face to face with death and found all was well. In that experience, I learned an important lesson; that one who had been the subject of converting grace and was the child of God, could, in the midst of the severest sufferings, fix the thoughts upon God and heavenly things and derive great comfort and peace."

Jackson then turned the focus of the conversation to the battle, commenting on the flanking maneuver: "Our movement yesterday was a great success. I think the most successful military movement of my life, but I expect to receive far more credit for it than I deserve. Most men will think that I had planned it all out from the first, but it was not so. I simply took advantage of circumstances as they were presented to me in the providence of God. I feel that his hand led me. Let us give him all the glory."[23]

Sensing that Jackson was beginning to tire from the visit, Smith politely asked Lacy to leave so the general could rest. As the pastor walked out of the tent, he noticed Jackson's amputated arm wrapped in a blanket and laid on the ground. Thinking it undignified for the arm of such an important person to be relegated to a mass burial, Lacy picked up the extremity and traveled to

---

21 Lacy, "Narrative."

22 Susan P. Lee, *Memoirs of William Nelson Pendleton* (Philadelphia, PA, 1893), 271.

23 Lacy, "Narrative."

Ruins of Wilderness Tavern in 1864 with the Ellwood homestead visible
in the distant background.
Library of Congress

his brother's estate, Ellwood, located a mile from Wilderness Tavern. There, Lacy buried the arm in the same family cemetery where Hotchkiss had placed the body of his friend, Boswell. In 1903, Jimmy Smith placed a stone marker for the arm in the cemetery that still exists today.[24]

24 Ibid. John S. Apperson also saw the arm on the ground as he walked over to the tent shortly after the surgery. In his diary on May 3, 1863, he wrote: "All was quiet and outside the tent lay the amputated arm wrapped up." See W. G. Bean, "Stonewall Jackson's Jolly Chaplain, Beverly Tucker Lacy," in *West Virginia History* (January 1968), 89. Much speculation has occurred over the years concerning the exact location of Jackson's arm. Archeological excavation of the marker site by the National Park Service in 1998 failed to discover any evidence of the arm. There is no doubt Lacy buried the arm in the cemetery,

Lieutenant Henry Kyd Douglas, another young Virginian on Jackson's staff, appeared at 11:00 a.m. to give Smith an update on the fighting around Chancellorsville. Relaying the news to Jackson, Smith described the valor exhibited by the Stonewall Brigade as it charged through the Union line amid Jeb Stuart's shouts of "Remember Jackson!" Expressing the pride he had for his old brigade, Jackson remarked, "Just like them to do so, just like them. They are a noble set of men." Smith told him the victory had come at a cost, though: their brigade commander had fallen. "Paxton? Paxton?" Jackson asked, referring to Brig. Gen. Frank "Bull" Paxton, a friend from his days in Lexington, Virginia. He had been killed in action, Smith disclosed. Closing his eyes and turning away, Jackson remained silent.[25]

*   *   *

Sixty miles south of Wilderness Tavern in Richmond, Virginia, Anna Jackson had just finished attending a worship service when the Reverend William Brown asked for a moment of her time. "Very sadly and feelingly," she recalled, "he informed me that the news had come that General Jackson had been wounded—severely, but it was hoped not dangerously." The painful shock she experienced at the moment was "better imagined than described."

A dispatch was immediately sent inquiring of the general's condition and asking whether Mrs. Jackson could come to the hospital. A response later in the day indicated her husband was doing well, but the way was not clear for her to journey north—passenger travel on the railroad had stopped due to Union cavalry raids in the area. Assured by railroad authorities that the tracks would be clear in a day or two, Anna's friends convinced her to wait instead of risking capture by traveling in a wagon.[26]

Back at Chancellorsville, General Lee had sent his own message to the hospital advising that Jackson be moved, if possible, to Guiney Station. He was concerned Federal forces would outflank the Confederate army in the Wilderness Tavern area and thereby capture Jackson. From the train station,

---

but Smith apparently placed the marker to indicate only the approximate location of its burial. See Appendix I for a more thorough discussion.

25 Smith, "Lt. Smith Narrative."

26 Jackson, *Life and Letters*, 462.

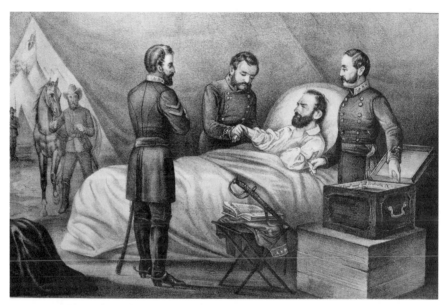

An 1872 Currier and Ives lithograph entitled "The Death of Stonewall Jackson."
Author's Collection

Lee reasoned, the wounded general could be quickly moved farther south if needed.

Jackson, however, did not want to leave if it would endanger his health. "I am not afraid of the enemy troubling me," he said. "I have always been kind to their wounded and they will be kind to me, I feel sure." In fact, Jackson, at the suggestion and urging of McGuire, had been the first in the war to recognize physicians as noncombatants. After the capture of several Union surgeons following the battle of Winchester in 1862, Jackson permitted the men to be released back to their units once they were finished caring for their own Federal wounded. The gesture was reciprocated on the Union side, and the action subsequently became the official policy of both the United States and Confederate governments.[27]

It was close to 8:00 p.m. that night before Hunter McGuire returned to the corps hospital. Checking in on the general, he was pleased to find the pain in his right side had disappeared and he appeared to be doing well.

27 McGuire, "Last Hours of Stonewall Jackson"; Samuel E. Lewis, "General T. J. Jackson (Stonewall) and his Medical Director, Hunter McGuire, M.D., at Winchester, May 1862," in *The Southern Practitioner* (October 1902), vol. 24, 553-564; *OR*, Series II, vol. 4, 44-46, 784.

Jackson was eager for more information about the battle and asked McGuire about minute details of which troops were engaged and how they had fared. When the surgeon reiterated the gallantry displayed by his old brigade, Jackson commented, "The men of that command will one day be proud to say to their children, 'I was one of the Stonewall Brigade.'" He then went on to deny any right to the name "Stonewall": "It belongs to the brigade and not at all to me."[28]

McGuire thought Jackson was stable enough for the move to Guiney Station the next morning, and informed the general that he planned on accompanying him. In response, Jackson said he "very much" wanted McGuire with him, but that it was not fair to the rest of the army. He knew it must have been difficult for McGuire to operate on a friend, and he thanked him for his care, but he could not permit him to come along: "You belong to the corps, Doctor, and not to me."[29]

Sandie Pendleton, however, was not about to stand by and let someone else care for Jackson, particularly when he knew the general preferred McGuire. He quietly left to inform General Lee of the situation. Later that night, Pendleton returned with an order written in Lee's own hand directing McGuire to turn his corps duties over to Black and to stay with the general as long as necessary. "General Lee has always been very kind to me," Jackson said after being told of the order. "I thank him."[30]

28 Smith, "Lt. Smith Narrative"; McGuire, "Last Hours of Stonewall Jackson"; McGuire, "Last Wound of the Late Gen. Jackson," 407-408.

29 McGuire, "Last Hours of Stonewall Jackson."

30 Ibid.; McGuire, "Last Wound of the Late Gen. Jackson," 408.

Chapter Eight

An Old Familiar Face

Stonewall Jackson slept well through the first full night following the amputation of his arm and awoke early on Monday morning May 4, 1863, ready for his long journey—27 miles—to Guiney Station. The plans were for him to stay at the comfortable home of Thomas Coleman Chandler, a "Christian gentleman" by Jackson's description, who owned and operated a 700-acre plantation called Fairfield that was located near the railroad station. Jackson had met the Chandler family the previous December when he and the Second Corps had camped on the grounds of the estate prior to the battle of Fredericksburg. During that time, the Chandlers offered Jackson the use of their large house as his headquarters, but the general politely refused, saying "he never wished to fare better than his soldiers." He remained instead in a tent within sight of the house and even declined to accept the special meals Mrs. Chandler repeatedly sent for his enjoyment.[1]

1 Lucy Chandler Pendleton to Edward T. Stuart, May 30, 1930, FSNMP, bound volume 188; R. L. C. Barrett, "Mrs. Pendleton Tells of Jackson's Passing Away at her Old Home," *Herald-Progress* (Ashland, VA), November 25, 1925. Hunter McGuire originally provided Hotchkiss with his handwritten account, "Last Hours of Stonewall Jackson," for

McGuire asked the officer in charge of the ambulance corps to provide "one of his most careful drivers" to handle the wagon for the ride to Guiney Station, and the detail was given to a 21-year-old Georgian named John J. Carson. After enlisting in the 12th Georgia Regiment at the start of the war, Carson had been wounded in 1861 and was serving on the ambulance corps until he was well enough to return to the front line. A mattress was placed in the back of Carson's ambulance to make the general's ride more comfortable, and by 6:00 a.m. all was ready for the trip to Fairfield.[2]

Under a small cavalry escort, the ambulance left Wilderness Tavern at a slow pace, with McGuire sitting in the wagon next to Jackson as Smith and Lacy rode alongside on horseback. A party of pioneers—the Civil War equivalent of modern-day combat engineers—traveled ahead of the ambulance. Led by Jed Hotchkiss, these men cleared the road of obstacles and asked other wagons along the way to move out of the road to make room for the ambulance. The callous teamsters they met along the road would initially refuse to make way for the ambulance until Hotchkiss told them it contained Jackson. Then, with hats in hand, the drivers would stand on the side of the road as the wagon passed, some weeping and others commenting, "I wish it was me, sir."[3]

The route to Guiney Station took them down the Brock Road past Todd's Tavern and through the community of Spotsylvania Court House. The road was in "bad shape," according to Carson, and when coming to a rough spot he could not avoid, he would alert McGuire, who "would place

---

publication in the book *Chancellorsville: Embracing the Operations of the Army of Northern Virginia from the First Battle of Fredericksburg to the Death of Lieutenant-General Jackson* (New York, NY, 1867) by Jed Hotchkiss and William Allan. In this early narrative, McGuire mistakenly indicated that the ride to Guiney Station occurred on Tuesday, May 5. Because McGuire used this account as a template for future writings, the chronological error persisted in several later publications. G. F. R. Henderson discovered the mistake while collecting information for his book *Stonewall Jackson and the American Civil War*. Henderson alerted Hotchkiss to the mistake, who then wrote to McGuire about the "important error," saying, "I do not see how this escaped the attention of Col. Allan or myself and how it has been so long unnoticed." See Jedediah Hotchkiss to Hunter McGuire, July 22, 1897, Hotchkiss Collection, reel 34, LC.

2   John J. Carson to Mary C. Higgs, January 20, 1916, copy in author's possession. Carson returned to action in 1864 and was wounded twice more before the end of the war. See Tom E. Sanders, "He is Dead, Yet He Liveth," *Civil War Times* (2008), vol. 46, issue 10, 38-39.

3   McGuire, "Last Hours of Stonewall Jackson"; Smith, "Lt. Smith Narrative"; Lacy, "Narrative"; Hotchkiss, *Make Me a Map of the Valley*, 140.

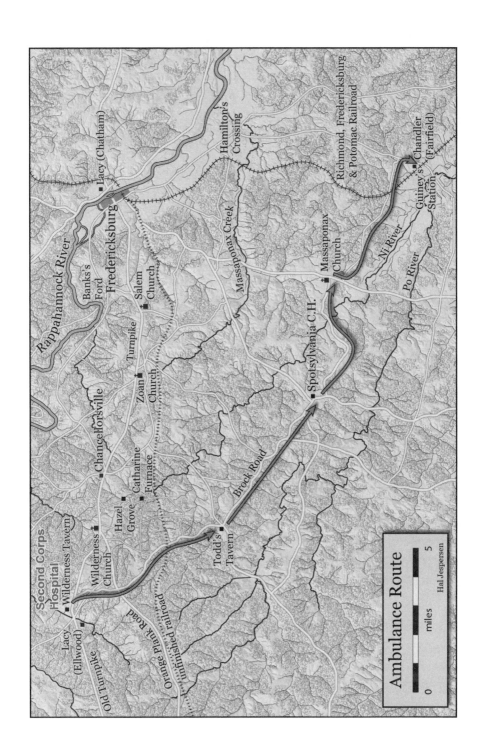

Ambulance Route

0   miles   5

Hal Jespersen

one hand on the general's breast and the other on his back in order to steady him." The weather was pleasant, though a bit warm, and a cheerful Jackson conversed freely and often during the trip. He commented that he felt "far more comfortable than he had a right to expect," and McGuire thought at the time that all "promised well for his case." Jackson hoped to rest at Fairfield for only a couple of days before proceeding by train to Ashland en route to his Lexington home, where he thought the "pure mountain air would soon heal his wounds."[4]

Along the way to Fairfield, Jackson discussed the battle of Chancellorsville and how his plans had been to take a position between the Federals and the river by cutting them off from the U.S. Ford and obliging them to attack him. "My men sometimes fail to drive the enemy from a position," he offered, "but they always fail to drive us away." He thought Hooker had devised an excellent strategy to defeat the Confederates, but had made a fatal mistake in sending away his cavalry: "It was that which enabled me to turn him, without his being aware of it, and to take him by his rear."[5]

Jackson spoke highly of Rodes—"he is a soldier"—and also praised the work of Col. Edward Willis of the 12th Georgia, Carson's old unit. As further commentary on the bravery of his officers, Jackson expressed the opinion that men should be promoted on the field for gallantry; as such actions "would be the greatest incentives to gallantry in others." He then spoke with deep regret of the deaths of Paxton and Boswell, believing they had been officers of great merit and promise.[6]

At some point during the long, slow ride, Jackson suffered from a small bout of nausea and asked for a wet towel to be placed over his stomach. McGuire saw no harm in the request, so he had Carson stop the ambulance at a roadside stream to obtain some cool water. McGuire said the general "expressed great relief" from the moist cloth, and with the surgeon dampening "it once or twice for him when it became dry," Jackson remained free of complaints for the remainder of the trip.

---

4 John J. Carson to Mary C. Higgs, January 20, 1916; McGuire, "Narrative"; Robert L. Dabney, *Life and Campaigns of Lieut-Gen. Thomas J. Jackson* (New York, NY, 1866), 711.

5 Dabney, *Life and Campaigns*, 713; McGuire, "Last Hours of Stonewall Jackson."

6 Ibid.

An 1872 photograph of the front of the outbuilding at Fairfield.
Author's Collection

As word spread along the way that Jackson was coming down the road, residents ran out to see him. "Along the whole route," McGuire wrote, "women rushed to the ambulance bringing all the poor delicacies they had and with tearful eyes, blessed him and prayed for his recovery." Near Spotsylvania Court House, the group stopped to eat and met a baggage wagon that happened to have mail for the general. Jackson wanted to save it for later reading and asked Smith to put the letters in his pocket until they arrived at Fairfield.[7]

The Chandler residence was a large, brick house with several outbuildings surrounded by fruit trees, vegetables gardens, and flowering shrubs. One hundred and fifty yards behind the main dwelling, a single track of the Richmond, Fredericksburg & Potomac Railroad stretched to Guiney Station, a quarter of a mile south of the homestead. Thomas and Mary

7   Ibid.; Smith, "Lt. Smith Narrative."

Present-day photograph of the right rear of outbuilding.
Window to Jackson's room is in the foreground.
Author's Collection

Chandler lived in the house along with their children, including an 11-year-old daughter, Lucy. An older son named Joseph was a physician who lived with his wife in a house near Fairfield.

Mary Chandler and Lucy were sitting on the front porch of the house around 4:00 p.m. when a courier swiftly rode up to inform them that Jackson had been wounded and was on his way by ambulance to stay at their home. After assuring the courier she would do all she could to accommodate the general, Mrs. Chandler and two slaves went to work turning the first-floor parlor into a bedroom, as the other rooms in the house were already occupied by several wounded soldiers from the battle of Chancellorsville.

When the ambulance was two miles from Fairfield, Tucker Lacy quickly rode ahead to check on the accommodations. Standing in the make-shift parlor bedroom, he noticed the coming and going of nurses attending the wounded and heard the trampling of feet in the rooms overhead.

"I do not think this will suit," the chaplain said to Mrs. Chandler. "There is too much noise." Doctor McGuire, Lacy informed her, wanted Jackson to be undisturbed during his recovery, and there was clearly too much activity in the house. Mary Chandler promised to keep the place quiet; however, realizing that would be impossible, Lacy inquired whether the small, frame structure he had noticed to the left of the main house was occupied. She told him the building was practically empty, as the interior had just been whitewashed. Lacy asked to see the inside.[8]

The one-and-a-half-story outbuilding consisted of several rooms on the ground floor that had been used as an office by Joseph Chandler when he first began practicing medicine. A small anteroom in the entry contained a staircase to the second floor and doors leading to three other rooms. The room to the back right of the entrance hall had a fireplace and a window that looked out onto the railroad track behind the plantation house. Inside the room, Lucy Chandler recalled, was a four-poster wooden bed of "the old-fashioned kind that you wind up with a rope." The building was isolated from the rest of the house yet easily accessible, seemingly ideal for the general. Lacy asked Mrs. Chandler to have the place "fitted up to receive him." Leaving her to complete the task, he mounted his horse and rode back to the meet the ambulance.[9]

Mary Chandler quickly covered the bed with blankets and arranged furniture in the building to make the rooms more comfortable. On the fireplace mantel, she placed a Gothic-styled pendulum clock that Jackson would be able to see while lying in bed. A recent thunderstorm had cooled the outside temperature, so, as a final measure, she lit a small fire in the room to take the edge off the evening chill.

It was close to 8:00 p.m. before the ambulance finally arrived at the Fairfield homestead. Waiting for them at the gate of a small wooden fence that separated the outbuilding from the front yard was the patriarch of the estate, Thomas C. Chandler. As Jackson was being removed from the ambulance, Chandler told the general he was glad to see him again, but sorry to hear he was wounded. Jackson thanked him for his hospitality and

8 Lucy Chandler Pendleton to Edward T. Stuart, May 30, 1930; *Herald-Progress* (Ashland, VA), November 25, 1925.

9 Ibid.; Lucy Chandler Pendleton to Edward T. Stuart, May 30, 1930; Smith, "Lt. Smith Narrative." Anna Jackson wrote in *Life and Letters of General Thomas J. Jackson* that it was "the surgeons" who decided to use the outbuilding because some of the wounded soldiers in the main house were suffering from erysipelas. As a result, subsequent writers often attributed the decision to McGuire, but it appears the room choice was made by Lacy before McGuire arrived at Fairfield.

Four-poster bed Jackson used at Fairfield.
Author's Collection

apologized for not being able to shake hands, as "one arm was gone and the right hand was wounded."[10]

Jackson was carried by stretcher into the building and gently placed in bed. McGuire then gave specific instructions that no one was to enter the room without permission except himself, Smith, and Jackson's servant Jim Lewis. Lacy, who was thereby denied unlimited access to the general, would later complain to an aide about the surgeon's restrictions on Jackson's conversations; the chaplain believed he could have talked to the general more "without injury to his wound."[11]

As the long day drew to a close, McGuire noted that the wearied Jackson drifted off to sleep, but not before drinking some tea and eating bread "with evident relish."

10 Lucy Chandler Pendleton to Edward T. Stuart, May 30, 1930.

11 Everard H. Smith, ed., "The Civil War Diary of Peter W. Hairston, Volunteer Aide to Major General Jubal A. Early, November 7–December 4, 1863," in *North Carolina Historical Review* (1990), vol. 67, issue 1, 59-86 (entry for November 18, 1863).

Although Jackson had tolerated the ride to Fairfield "very well," McGuire was concerned about the possibility of a secondary hemorrhage developing in the stump as a result of the rough travel, so the cautious surgeon "sat up with him the whole of this night." In the end, Jackson slept peacefully and awoke Tuesday morning "safe" and "quite comfortable," according to the physician.[12]

That morning, May 5, Jimmy Smith sent a short telegram from Guiney Station to Virginia's governor and Jackson's friend, John Letcher:

> "Genl. Jackson is here. He has lost his left arm and is doing remarkably well. Let Mrs. J remain until further arrangements."[13]

Jed Hotchkiss also came by for a visit and found the general "cheerful." Jackson was slightly annoyed by the cold he had caught the night before his wounding, but felt it was of no particular importance. When the cartographer asked for orders, Jackson instructed him to report to General Lee, as the commander was sure to need his services as the battle continued. As Hotchkiss left, Jackson expressed a desire to see more staff members and friends, but McGuire, believing the general still needed rest, advised against it.

Lacy, however, was permitted in at 10:00 a.m. to pray with Jackson, using bible verses personally selected by the general. Jackson continued to express "faith and hope in his Redeemer" and believed he would fully recover from his wounds, as God still had work for him to do in defense of his country. When Lacy related that he had heard Hooker was entrenching north of Chancellorsville, Jackson replied, "That is bad, very bad."[14]

Jackson anticipated starting his train journey to Lexington the next day and initially asked Lacy to accompany him. Upon further reflection, however, Jackson decided otherwise, believing—as he had when McGuire

---

12 McGuire, "Last Wound of the Late Gen. Jackson," 409; McGuire, "Last Hours of Stonewall Jackson"; McGuire, "Narrative."

13 *Fourth Annual Report of the Library Board of the Virginia State Library 1906-1907* (Richmond, VA, 1907), 99.

14 Hotchkiss, *Make Me a Map of the Valley*, 141; McGuire, "Last Hours of Stonewall Jackson"; McGuire, "Narrative"; Cooke, *Stonewall Jackson: A Military Biography*, 442; *Richmond (VA) Enquirer*, May 13, 1863; Lacy, "Narrative"; Dabney, *Life and Campaigns*, 713.

wanted to come to Fairfield—that it would set a bad example of "self-gratification" to the troops, so Lacy should instead stay at his post preaching to the army.[15]

The standard treatment for post-amputation wounds during the Civil War included wet dressings over the site in an attempt to both decrease inflammation and absorb any discharge that might leak from the incision. The most frequent method of "water dressings" used at the time involved applying a cotton cloth over the wound and running a lamp wick from the dressing to a suspended bucket or bowl filled with water. The dressing and wick was then covered with a layer of waxed cloth or india rubber, followed by another layer of cloth bandage to hold the dressings in place. The apparatus would cause a constant stream of water to flow down the wick via capillary action to the dressing placed directly against the wound.

This method required the dressings to be changed at least daily. While completing the task on Tuesday, McGuire informed Jackson that his wounds were doing very well. Pleased at the report, Jackson was confident their healthy appearance indicated that he would not be absent from the field for very long.[16]

Farther to the south in Richmond that day, Joseph Morrison was just reaching Anna Jackson. Having left Wilderness Tavern on horseback early Sunday morning, Morrison had taken a circuitous route to Guiney Station, where he boarded a Richmond-bound train that was filled with wounded soldiers from the battle of Chancellorsville.

After arriving in Ashland, about 15 miles north of Richmond, the train was suddenly seized by a company of raiding Union cavalry. After inspecting the cars and finding only wounded soldiers, a Federal officer ordered all those who could walk off the train before proceeding to collect the names of the wounded men for parole. After quickly burning his pocket diary to keep it from falling into the hands of the enemy, Morrison exited the train in line with the other Confederates. Due to a lack of vigilance on the part of the Union soldiers, he was eventually able to make an escape and set off for Richmond on foot. He traveled most of the night before being warned by helpful citizens that Union cavalry controlled the roads toward the

---

15 Susan Lee, *Memoirs of William Nelson Pendleton*, 271.

16 *Richmond (VA) Enquirer*, May 13, 1863; McGuire, "Last Wound of the Late Gen. Jackson," 409.

capital. Compelled to wait another day, it was Tuesday morning before he was able to enter the city and find Anna at the home of Moses Hoge.

Anna Jackson learned from her brother the particulars of her husband's wounds and the amputation of his arm. Morrison reassured his sister that the general "was doing as well as possible under the circumstances, and was brave and cheerful in spirit." She wanted to leave Richmond and head north immediately, but Morrison's arduous journey demonstrated the importance of waiting until the roads and railway were clear of enemy soldiers.[17]

*   *   *

When dawn arrived on Wednesday, May 6, it was greeted by a cold rain that had started the previous night and would continue throughout most of the day. Jackson had planned to leave Guiney Station that morning to begin his journey home to Lexington, but the trip was postponed until the weather became more favorable.

From a medical standpoint, Jackson continued to do "remarkably well," according to McGuire. He "ate heartily for one in his condition," and his attitude continued to be one of optimism and cheer. All meals for the general and his staff were gladly provided by Mrs. Chandler, and the food was frequently accompanied by milk, a long-time staple of Jackson's diet that he used for managing his chronic dyspepsia.[18]

Post-operative infections were a dire complication of amputations during the Civil War, a time when antibiotics did not yet exist, sterile technique was unappreciated, and the germ theory of disease transmission had yet to be advanced in medical science. The three most common, and often fatal, wound site infections of the period were erysipelas, gangrene, and pyemia, or "blood poisoning." Each disease presented its own unique set of signs and symptoms, and most military surgeons vigilantly monitored the surgical site for changes that heralded the onset of one of these potentially deadly infections.

17 Joseph G. Morrison, "Stonewall Jackson at Chancellorsville," *CV* (May 1905); Joseph G. Morrison to Robert Dabney, October 29, 1863; Joseph G. Morrison to Spier Whitaker, June 27, 1900; Jackson, *Life and Letters*, 463.

18 *Richmond (VA) Enquirer*, May 13, 1863; McGuire, "Last Wound of the Late Gen. Jackson," 409; Lucy Chandler Pendleton to Edward T. Stuart, May 30, 1930.

Bedside clinical notes McGuire took of Jackson's recovery were lost when his medical wagon was captured during the 1865 battle of Waynesboro, Virginia, but the surgeon emphasized in later writings that Jackson's wounds never displayed any signs of infection. For instance, during a dressing change on Wednesday, McGuire noted that the general's wounds were doing "very well," as healing had taken place "to some extent in the stump" with "healthy granulations" covering the incision site. The right hand wound was also healing well and gave Jackson "little pain." McGuire covered the wounds with "simple lint and water dressings," followed by placement of a short splint on the general's right hand to immobilize the broken bones.[19]

As McGuire was finishing the dressing change that day, Jackson took the time to comment on his wounds to Jimmy Smith, who was standing nearby. "Many would regard them as a great misfortune; I regard them as one of the blessings of my life."

"All things work together for good to them that love God," Smith replied, quoting one of the general's favorite bible verses.

"Yes!" Jackson exclaimed. "That's it! That's it!"[20]

The most significant news of the day was the reported disappearance of the Army of the Potomac. During the night, Hooker had retreated across the Rappahannock River, ending the battle of Chancellorsville with a Confederate victory.

Although the end of the fighting removed any worry of Jackson being captured, the heavy burden and constant strain of caring for the wounded general were beginning to take their toll on Hunter McGuire. The young physician had barely slept for three consecutive nights, and he was now feeling "quite sick" himself. Since Jackson was stable and improving, it seemed to be a good time for McGuire to try to get some rest of his own. Leaving the general under the watchful care of Jim Lewis and Tucker Lacy, the exhausted surgeon spent the night asleep on a nearby lounge.[21]

Around 1:00 a.m., Jackson awoke and complained of not feeling well—the nausea that had affected him during the ambulance ride on

19 McGuire, "Last Wound of the Late Gen. Jackson," 409.

20 Ibid., 410.

21 McGuire, "Last Hours of Stonewall Jackson."

Monday had returned. He wanted to use the water cure again, and asked Lewis to get a wet towel and place it on his stomach. The servant hesitated, suggesting that he wake McGuire first to see whether the treatment was appropriate. Well aware that the young physician was getting his first full sleep in days, Jackson refused to allow him to be awakened. Reluctantly, Lewis obtained a wet cloth and placed it on the general's stomach. This time, however, the water therapy had no effect. Not only did the nausea continue unabated throughout the night, but the right side pain he had experienced the day after his wounding also reappeared.

The sharp pain in Jackson's chest steadily increased to the point where he struggled to breathe normally. Around dawn, he finally allowed Lewis to awaken McGuire, who then found the general "suffering with great pain in his side and difficulty of breathing." While turning down Jackson's clothes to examine him, McGuire noticed that the bed was damp, prompting Lewis to inform him of the persistent nausea and the unsuccessful use of the wet towel.

A thorough examination by McGuire revealed the source of the symptoms: Jackson was suffering from "pleuro-pneumonia of the right side." Pneumonia was a well-known—and deadly—illness during the Civil War. Over 60,000 cases of the infection were documented during the conflict's four years, with a mortality rate of 24 percent, making "inflammation of the lungs and pleura" the third most common cause of death due to disease. The pleura, a thin membrane covering the lung surface and the inside of the chest cavity, is richly supplied with pain-sensing nerves that are not found within the lungs themselves. When an infection reaches the surface of a lung, the sharp pain of pleurisy is often felt. Since Jackson had both pneumonia and pleurisy, McGuire used the period term "pleuro-pneumonia" to describe his condition.[22]

Rumors would eventually circulate through the army that Jackson's pneumonia was caused by the use of the wet towels to treat his nausea on Wednesday night. McGuire dispelled such rumors in later writings, stating, "The disease came on too soon after the application of the wet cloths, to admit of the supposition, once believed, that it was induced by them."

22 Ibid.; McGuire, "Last Wound of the Late Gen. Jackson," 410; Charles Smart, *The Medical and Surgical History of the War of the Rebellion* (Washington, D.C., 1888), pt. 3, vol. I, 751-810.

Instead, McGuire and colleagues maintained the pneumonia was a complication of a pulmonary contusion, or bruised lung, that Jackson suffered when he fell from the litter the night of his wounding. "Contusion of the lung," McGuire wrote, "with extravasation of blood in his chest, was probably produced by the fall referred to, and shock and loss of blood prevented any ill effects until reaction had been well established, and then inflammation ensued."[23]

McGuire instantly realized the danger presented by pneumonia: the illness carried a mortality rate nearly twice that of the amputation he had performed on Jackson. In the pre-antibiotic era of medicine, effective treatments for the infection were limited, but McGuire would use all the standard and accepted medical therapies of the time. He started by administering opium, often in the form of morphine, to control the pain Jackson was experiencing and to help him rest more comfortably. While the morphine would be successful in relieving the general's discomfort, it would also affect his mental alertness, leading to a stupor that would contribute to the delirium he would eventually develop from the pneumonia.

McGuire also performed wet cupping, a form of superficial bleeding, after the appropriate instruments were obtained from the nearby house of Dr. Joseph A. Chandler. Wet cupping was a common technique used to draw blood to the surface of the skin by first placing a glass vessel over the affected lung and heating it to create an internal vacuum, causing the raising of a blister. The blister was then cut open with an instrument known as a scarificator, followed by reapplication of the cup. The suction from the cup would subsequently withdraw anywhere from two to four ounces of blood from the open blister. The liberal use of cathartics, or medications to purge the gastrointestinal tract, were another pre-antibiotic treatment for pneumonia; as a result, Jackson was given repeated oral doses of mercury as a laxative and antimony to induce vomiting.[24]

The seriousness of Jackson's illness necessitated the services of more than one physician, so McGuire sent Tucker Lacy to request the help of

---

23 McGuire, "Last Wound of the Late Gen. Jackson," 410; McGuire, "Last Hours of Stonewall Jackson"; McGuire, "Death of Stonewall Jackson," 160-161.

24 Joseph A. Chandler to R. A. Lancaster, Jr., October 16, 1894, Thomas J. Jackson Collection, MOC; Smart, *The Medical and Surgical History of the War of the Rebellion*, 809.

Samuel B. Morrison, chief surgeon of Maj. Gen. Jubal A. Early's division and distant relative to Anna Jackson; Morrison had served as the Jacksons' family physician prior to the start of the war.

En route to finding Morrison, Lacy stopped at General Lee's headquarters to inform the commander that Jackson's condition had suddenly worsened. Although concerned at the news, Lee stated he was confident God would see to the general's recovery, adding, "Give General Jackson my affectionate regards and say to him: He has lost his left arm, but I my right arm. Tell him to get well and come back to me as soon as he can."[25]

*　*　*

With the tracks of the Richmond, Fredericksburg, & Potomac Railroad repaired and Union cavalry out of the immediate area, Anna Jackson was finally able to board an armed train to Guiney Station. She was accompanied by her infant daughter Julia, a nurse named Aunt Hetty, and her brother Joseph Morrison. The group arrived at Fairfield where Jimmy Smith greeted them shortly after noon on May 7.

Anna immediately inquired of her husband's condition, and by the way the young lieutenant replied "pretty well," she could tell something was wrong. The tone and manner of his response betrayed the gravity of the situation, and her "heart sank like lead." She wanted to see him immediately, but was told McGuire was busy changing the dressings and she would have to wait until he was finished.[26]

While pacing anxiously along the porch, Anna suddenly became "horrified" by the sight of soldiers digging in a grave near the house, exhuming a coffin, and placing it on the ground next to the freshly dug hole. She was told the casket contained the body of the Jacksons' friend Frank Paxton and was being taken back to Lexington for final burial. Anna knew Paxton's young wife, and the realization that her friend was now a widow had a profound effect upon her own emotional state. She would later recall that her "own heart almost stood still under the weight and apprehension" of

25 Lacy, "Narrative." Lee's phraseology about losing his right arm is also documented in a soldier's letter home within days of the incident. See John A. Crawford to sister, May 12, 1863, Crawford Family Papers, University of South Carolina.

26 Jackson, *Life and Letters*, 464.

Dr. Samuel Morrison.
Virginia Historical Society (1972.13.19)

the awareness, and that she felt the "ghastly spectacle was a most unfitting preparation for my entrance into the presence of my stricken husband."[27]

Jackson had requested some lemonade, so Smith tried to redirect Anna's nervous energy by suggesting she occupy her time mixing the drink. Although her mind was understandably more focused on seeing her ailing husband than on making lemonade, she tried nonetheless. Smith took a glass

27 Ibid.

of the newly made drink to Jackson, who took one sip and stated, "You didn't mix this, it is too sweet. Take it back."[28]

When Anna was finally allowed into the sick room, Jackson was lying in bed with his eyes closed. She quietly walked to the bed, leaned over, and gently kissed him. A smile spread across his face when he opened his eyes and saw his wife beside him. "I am very glad to see you looking so bright," he said to her. His appearance, though, was in such contrast to the way he had looked eight days previously when she had last seen him that her own smile quickly faded at the sight. With his "face sunken, complexion bad, and respiration terribly difficult," Anna wrote, "he looked like a dying man."

As Anna's anxiety and sadness intensified, he softly said to her, "My darling, you must cheer up, and not wear a long face. I love cheerfulness and brightness in a sickroom." Finding it impossible to resist the drowsiness of the morphine, Jackson then faded off to sleep.[29]

The general spent the remainder of the afternoon with Anna at his side while he drifted in and out of consciousness, at one time calling out in his stupor, "Major Pendleton send in and see if there is higher ground back of Chancellor's!" While awake, he was too nauseated to ingest much nourishment, so McGuire sent Jim Lewis to the house to ask Mrs. Chandler for some thin "ice cream made of skim milk flavored with a little vanilla," hoping the general would tolerate a light diet.[30]

Dr. Sam Morrison first arrived at the house that evening around 5:00 p.m. and noted that Jackson was breathing "badly" and "suffering much pain." As his former physician entered the room, Jackson raised his right arm and proclaimed, "There's an old familiar face."[31]

Although confident of the diagnosis and treatment plan, McGuire and Morrison thought an expert opinion on Jackson's condition might be beneficial. They decided to seek the help of Dr. David H. Tucker at the Medical College of Virginia in Richmond, a well-respected physician who was considered an authority on pneumonia. Additionally, Anna Jackson

28 Smith, "Lt. Smith Narrative."

29 Anna Jackson to Laura Arnold, September 12, 1864, VMI; Jackson, "Narrative"; Jackson, *Life and Letters*, 465.

30 Lacy, "Narrative"; Lucy Chandler Pendleton to Edward T. Stuart, May 30, 1930.

31 Samuel B. Morrison to uncle, May 13, 1863, Florida Atlantic University (FAU); Samuel Morrison, "Narrative," Dabney-Jackson Collection, box 2, LVA.

needed help caring for young Julia, as she was determined to spend as much time as possible next to her husband; she suggested her friend Susan Hoge, another resident of Richmond. As a result, Jimmy Smith departed for the city that evening tasked with bringing Dr. Tucker, Mrs. Hoge, and more lemons back to Fairfield.[32]

As Thursday, May 7, 1863, came to a close, Jackson's chest pain started to diminish and his condition actually improved—to the extent, McGuire said, that "hopes were again entertained of his recovery." Jackson was pleased to have Anna at his bedside, telling her that evening, "You are one of the most precious little wives in the world." Although he slept somewhat fitfully that night, he had no further complaints of chest discomfort or nausea.[33]

Jackson's clinical improvement lasted into a misty Friday morning. His pain was gone and Anna thought his mind "more rational." He told Sam Morrison that he felt better and believed he would get well, as "God has yet a work for me to perform." McGuire was also pleased to find no signs of a developing infection in Jackson's wounds, noting during the day's dressing change that the "process of healing was still going on." Engaging in a religious discussion with McGuire at the time, Jackson asked the surgeon whether he thought diseased persons "healed by the miraculous touch of the Savior" ever suffered again from the same malady. McGuire thought such a recurrence would be impossible, and Jackson agreed with his physician, believing the "healing virtue of the Redeemer was too potent." Then, after a brief pause, Jackson looked upward and exclaimed, "Oh, for infinite power!"[34]

With Jackson improving, Sam Morrison felt comfortable leaving Fairfield at 11:00 a.m. to attend the wounded at his own division hospital. Meanwhile, Smith returned from his errands in Richmond and entered the

---

32 Smith, "Lt. Smith Narrative"; McGuire, "Last Hours of Stonewall Jackson"; Anna Jackson to Laura Arnold, September 12, 1864.

33 McGuire, "Last Wound of the Late Gen. Jackson," 410; Anna Jackson to Laura Arnold, September 12, 1864.

34 Anna Jackson to Laura Arnold, September 12, 1864; Samuel B. Morrison to uncle, May 13, 1863; McGuire, "Last Wound of the Late Gen. Jackson," 411; Dabney, *Life and Campaigns*, 720.

room just as Jackson was in the middle of another discussion of a religious nature.

"Mr. Smith," Jackson asked the divinity student, "what were the headquarters of the Christians after the crucifixion?"

The young lieutenant replied that before Rome was established as the headquarters, there existed only "centers of influence," such as Antioch and Iconium.

Intrigued by the answer, Jackson instructed, "Mr. Smith, I wish you would get the map and show me precisely where Iconium was."

When Smith replied that no map of the area was currently at hand, Jackson offered, "Yes, sir. You will find it in the atlas in my old trunk." After searching the trunk but finding no map, Smith suggested the general had perhaps left it in his portable desk.

"Yes, I left it in my box," Jackson acknowledged, then added, "Mr. Smith, I wish you would examine into that matter and report to me."[35]

Optimism about Jackson's eventual recovery, however, was short-lived. Late in the afternoon, both his fever and breathing difficulty returned. As Dr. Tucker had not yet arrived from Richmond, McGuire solicited the opinions of two other military surgeons, Drs. Robert J. Breckenridge and J. Philip Smith. While both concurred with the diagnosis of pneumonia, Breckenridge suggested a blister placed over the affected lung might afford additional relief. Medical blisters of the period were typically a six by eight inch plaster of a caustic substance such as cantharides or croton oil that blistered the skin, intended to stimulate healing and draw the infection out of the lung and to the surface.[36]

Although he remained free of chest pain through the rest of the evening, Jackson's "prostration" increased and he complained to McGuire of "a feeling of great exhaustion." Anna asked that evening whether he wanted to see Julia, but he declined, saying he would prefer to wait until he felt better. He also refused her attempts to draw him into more conversation by

35 Ibid.; Smith, "Lt. Smith Narrative."

36 Breckenridge was the Inspector of Camps and Hospitals for the Army of Northern Virginia; Smith was a physician from Virginia who was with McGuire at the Winchester Medical College prior to the war. The latter was working as a physician in Confederate general hospitals.

reminding her that the doctors had advised he should remain quiet, though adding, "My darling, you are very much loved."[37]

Sam Morrison arrived back at Fairfield that evening to find Jackson's "delirium more constant and his strength failing, though when his attention was called, he seemed to recognize all persons present, and understood everything spoken to him." Jackson spent Friday night in a restless sleep, once calling out in a daze, "Tell Major Hawks to send forward provisions to the men." While tending to him during the night, Sam Morrison woke the general at one point to give him a dose of medicine, asking first, "Will you take this?"

"Do your duty," Jackson replied, "do your duty."[38]

37 McGuire, "Last Wound of the Late Gen. Jackson," 411; McGuire, "Last Hours of Stonewall Jackson"; Jackson, "Narrative"; Anna Jackson to Laura Arnold, September 12, 1864.

38 Jackson, "Narrative"; Samuel B. Morrison to uncle, May 13, 1863.

Chapter Nine

The Shade of the Trees

The morning of Saturday, May 9, 1863, dawned warm and clear over the Chandler plantation near Guiney Station, Virginia. Although the gray, overcast skies and cool temperatures outside had given way to a more pleasant environment, the atmosphere inside the small, frame building near the main house remained dreary. Seven days ago, Stonewall Jackson, already ill with a head cold, had nearly bled to death after being shot three times by his own men in a friendly fire accident. His removal from the field was complicated by a severe fall from the litter that resulted in a bruised right lung. He underwent amputation of his left arm five hours later and, the next day, was transported by wagon 27 miles to Fairfield, where he now lay battling a pneumonia that had developed in the injured lung. Despite the dedicated, around-the-clock medical care Jackson had received, it was becoming increasingly obvious to the physicians that his illness was fatal.

Although the general was free of pain and breathing a little easier, McGuire noted that Jackson was "hourly growing weaker." In a Saturday letter to his sister, Jimmy Smith wrote that Jackson was worse that morning and that his condition was "sinking." Dr. David Tucker, an expert in pneumonia, arrived from Richmond that day, examined Jackson, and concurred with the diagnosis and treatment. McGuire remained confident that "all that human skill could devise" was being done "to stay the hand of death."[1]

Tucker's presence brought the total to five doctors who had been involved in Jackson's care since he arrived at Fairfield, an occurrence that did not escape the general's notice.

"I see from the number of physicians that you think my condition dangerous," Jackson said to McGuire that morning, "but I thank God, if it is His will, that I am ready to go."[2]

Later that afternoon, Jackson asked to see Lacy. McGuire and the other physicians tried to dissuade him, believing the conversation would be too tiring, but he was so persistent in the request that they deemed it wise to appease him. When Lacy entered the room, Jackson asked the chaplain whether he was "endeavoring to further the matter of which he had spoken to him" concerning plans of "promoting the Sabbath observance" among the soldiers. Despite the pastor's assurances that he had done so, Jackson, as the physicians had predicted, continued to engage Lacy in a lengthy discussion on the topic.[3]

By evening, Jackson was becoming progressively fatigued and feverish. At one point, while Anna was wiping sweat from his forehead, he opened his eyes and noticed tears on her cheeks. "Anna, none of that, none of that," he softly chided her. Asking her to not "put on a long face" on his account, he went on: "Pray for me, but always remember in your prayers to use the petition, 'Thy will be done.'" Trying to find other ways to comfort him, she asked whether he would like to hear some Psalms read from the Old Testament. His initial response was that he was too tired to listen, but then he quickly changed his mind: "Yes, we must never refuse that. Get the Bible and read them."[4]

---

1   McGuire, "Last Wound of the Late Gen. Jackson," 411; McGuire, "Last Hours of Stonewall Jackson"; James P. Smith to sister, May 9, 1863, Thomas J. Jackson Collection, MOC.

2   McGuire, "Last Hours of Stonewall Jackson."

3   Jackson, "Narrative."

4   Samuel Morrison, "Narrative," Dabney-Jackson Collection, LVA; Samuel B. Morrison to uncle, May 13, 1863; Jackson, *Life and Letters*, 466.

Sam Morrison would tell Jackson later that night that it was possible he might not survive the pneumonia. Trying to remain optimistic, Jackson replied, "I think I shall be better by morning."[5]

During his time at Hamilton's Crossing prior to the battle, Jackson had enjoyed engaging the "musical members of his staff" in hymn singing every Sunday evening. Now, as his restlessness increased during the night, Jackson requested that his wife and others around sing the most spiritual pieces they could select. Anna and her brother Joseph began by singing "Harwell," followed by several of his other favorite hymns. They concluded, at Jackson's request, with Isaac Watt's verse based on the 51st Psalm and sung to the tune of the "Old Hundredth":

> Show pity, Lord, O Lord, forgive,
> Let a repenting rebel live;
> Are not thy mercies large and free?
> May not a sinner trust in thee?[6]

Jackson would get little sleep during the night, dozing intermittently as Smith sat up until 2:00 a.m. sponging his head with cool water. Anytime the aide happened to stop, Jackson would open his eyes and ask him to continue: "Go on Mr. Smith, it is good," he would say.[7]

The next morning, Sunday, May 10, 1863, there were "no grounds for hope," as Sam Morrison wrote in a letter to his uncle. McGuire and the other physicians realized that Jackson's exhaustion and weakness had progressed to a point at which their beloved general would not survive another day.[8]

Tucker Lacy wanted to remain with Jackson that morning, but the general's selfless concern for his soldiers' well-being remained constant, and he instructed the chaplain to return to camp and hold Sunday worship for the army as usual. Before the service, General Lee asked Lacy for an update on Jackson's condition, and the pastor informed him that the situation

---

5   Samuel Morrison, "Narrative."

6   Jackson, *Life and Letters*, 466; Jackson, "Narrative."

7   Smith, "Lt. Smith Narrative."

8   Samuel B. Morrison to uncle, May 13, 1863.

appeared hopeless. "Surely, Jackson must recover," a concerned Lee replied, "God will not take him from us now that we need him so much."[9]

With Lee, A. P. Hill, and 1,800 soldiers from Jackson's corps in attendance, Lacy preached a moving Sunday service based on the scripture, "All things work together for good to them that love God." Afterward, Lee approached Lacy again and expressed his belief that the prayers for Jackson's recovery would be answered, adding, "When you return, I trust you will find him better. When a suitable occasion offers, tell him that I prayed for him last night as I never prayed, I believe, for myself."[10]

Although Fairfield was not far from Lee's headquarters, the commanding general never saw Jackson during his illness. The wounding had been a troubling event for Lee, and his most noted biographer, Douglas Southall Freeman, believes he avoided visiting Jackson out of concern he would be unable to control his emotions. Focused work and ardent prayer, in Lee's mind, were the best solution for dealing with the painful situation.[11]

Despite the hopes and prayers of so many, Jackson's life continued to fade away at Fairfield. When it became evident by 10:00 a.m. that her husband could not be expected to survive the day, Anna was taken into another room by Sam Morrison and quietly informed that death was imminent. Maintaining her composure despite the "agony of that announcement," Anna asked whether she could tell her husband, as she felt sure he would want to know. She reflected on his past insistence that he was willing to die at any time if it was God's will, but he would desire to have a few hours' notice.[12]

Anna returned to the room, knelt down beside her husband's bed, and gently called his name. "Do you know that the doctors say you must very soon be in heaven?" she asked. Jackson, not fully awake, uncomprehendingly stared at her. "Do you know that in a very few hours, you will be with your Savior?" she posed again. Jackson remained silent. "If

---

9   Jackson, *Life and Letters*, 467; Lacy, "Narrative."

10 Ibid.; Hotchkiss, *Make Me a Map of the Valley*, 142.

11 Douglas Southall Freeman, *R. E. Lee: A Biography*, 4 vols. (New York, NY, 1934), vol. 2, 561.

12 McGuire, "Last Hours of Stonewall Jackson"; Jackson, "Narrative"; Samuel B. Morrison to uncle, May 13, 1863.

God wills you to go today, do you not feel willing to acquiesce in his allotment?"

"I prefer it," he finally answered, and then with added emphasis, repeated, "I prefer it."

"Before the day closes," she told him, "you will be with the blessed Savior in his glory."

"I shall be an infinite gainer to be translated," he replied.[13]

Anna asked whether he wanted her and the baby to live with her father in North Carolina. "Yes, back to your father," he replied. "You have a kind, good father, but our heavenly father is better than all." His mental alertness began to fade again, but Anna had more questions that needed answering. She asked where he wished to be buried.

"Charlotte . . . Charlottesville," he mumbled. Surprised at the answer, she asked whether he did not wish to be buried in Lexington. "Yes, Lexington," he whispered, "in my own plot." Anna then wanted to know whether he had any messages for his sister, Laura. "I am too much exhausted," he offered, "I have a great deal to say to you but this is no occasion for it now."[14]

Jackson rested quietly for nearly an hour and was more alert when he awoke around 11:00 a.m. Anna wanted to be sure he had comprehended the previous discussion and asked again whether he understood that "before the sun went down he would be with his Savior."

"Oh, no," he responded, "you are frightened, my child, death is not so near. I may yet recover."

Crying bitterly, Anna fell upon his bed and told him again that the doctors said there was no hope. After a moment's silence, Jackson said, "Call Doctor McGuire, let us know what he says about it."

McGuire, standing in the anteroom, entered the sick room when Anna called. "Doctor," Jackson asked him, "Anna says you have told her that I am to die today. Is it true?" The young physician sadly confirmed the prognosis. Jackson, turning his eyes toward the ceiling, gazed upward "in intense thought" for several seconds before stating, "Very good, very good. It is all

13 Jackson, "Narrative"; Anna Jackson to Laura Arnold, September 12, 1864.

14 McGuire, "Last Wound of the Late Gen. Jackson," 411; Jackson, *Life and Letters*, 470; Anna Jackson to Laura Arnold, September 12, 1864.

Mantel clock in Jackson's room at Fairfield.
Author's Collection

right." He then turned his attention to Anna and tried to console her by quoting passages from scripture.[15]

With Jackson awake and alert, his daughter Julia was brought into the room by Mrs. Hoge. It had been a short 20 days since the general walked onto the train at Guiney Station and laid eyes upon his infant daughter for the first time. Upon opening his eyes and seeing her again, the same broad smile

15 McGuire, "Last Wound of the Late Gen. Jackson," 411-412; McGuire, "Last Hours of Stonewall Jackson."

that had crossed his face at that time reappeared. "Little darling," he said fondly, "sweet one."

She was placed on the bed next to him, and the smiling infant cooed as he reached up and caressed her with his splinted hand. Calling her his "little comforter," he marveled at her being such a "bright baby." Julia remained beside him for several minutes before being reluctantly carried out of the room. Jackson took a moment before she left to close his eyes, raise his hand in the air, and offer a silent prayer over his daughter. The tenderness of the moment overwhelmed many in the room. "Tears were shed over that dying bed by strong men who were unused to weep," Anna recalled.[16]

As the mantel clock slowly and agonizingly ticked off the passing time, Jackson's mind alternated between moments of lucidity and delirium. During one of his rational periods, McGuire offered him a drink of brandy mixed with water. Jackson refused it: "It will only delay my departure, and do no good; I want to preserve my mind, if possible, to the last."[17]

Sandie Pendleton came into the room around noon and the general recognized him instantly. "Who was preaching at headquarters today?" he asked the young aide. Pendleton responded that Reverend Lacy had delivered the morning sermon and that the entire army was praying for him. "Thank you," he said, "they are very kind." After a moment's pause, he added, "It is the Lord's Day. My wish is fulfilled. I have always desired to die on Sunday."[18]

An hour later Jackson was progressively growing weaker and his delirium more frequent. "His mind now began to fail and wander," McGuire wrote, "and he frequently talked as if in command upon the field, giving orders in his old way, then the scene shifted and he was at the old mess table, going through conversations with members of his staff; now with his wife and child, now at prayers with his military family."[19]

---

16 McGuire, "Last Hours of Stonewall Jackson"; Jackson, "Narrative"; Jackson, *Life and Letters*, 470; Samuel B. Morrison to uncle, May 13, 1863.

17 McGuire, "Last Hours of Stonewall Jackson"; McGuire, "Last Wound of the Late Gen. Jackson," 412.

18 McGuire, "Last Hours of Stonewall Jackson"; McGuire, "Last Wound of the Late Gen. Jackson," 412; Samuel B. Morrison to uncle, May 13, 1863.

19 McGuire, "Last Hours of Stonewall Jackson"; McGuire, "Last Wound of the Late Gen. Jackson," 412.

At 1:30 p.m., McGuire somberly told Anna that her husband had only two hours to live. Kneeling beside him, she softly relayed to him that his time of departure was near. "Very good," he feebly responded. "It is all right."[20]

Jimmy Smith entered the room at 2:30 p.m. and stood silently by as Jackson slipped into a semi-comatose state. "Order A. P. Hill to prepare for action," Jackson suddenly called out, "Pass the infantry to the front. Tell Maj. Hawks. . . ." then the sentence trailed off as Jackson fell back into unconsciousness.[21]

The physical and emotional toll of the past week finally hit Hunter McGuire. The realization that all his knowledge and formidable skills had been unable to save the life of a close friend was almost too much for him to bear. "I left the room then," McGuire recalled, "unable in my enfeebled condition to restrain my grief at seeing him die."[22]

For several minutes, Jackson continued to intermittently mumble disconnected words. Then, very clearly and with "an expression as if of relief," he quietly remarked, "Let us cross over the river and rest under the shade of the trees."[23]

Those immortal words would be Jackson's last, as his breathing became increasingly shallow over the ensuing minutes. His life was slipping away, but Anna refused to let go. She called out to Dr. Tucker, "Doctor, can't you do something more?"

"No, madam," he solemnly replied, "human power can do no more."[24]

The sound of his wife's desperate voice momentarily brought Jackson back from the brink of death. He opened his eyes and lovingly looked into Anna's tearful face. At that moment the clock on the mantel struck 3:15 p.m., and Stonewall Jackson slowly closed his eyes forever.[25]

---

20 Ibid.

21 Smith, "Lt. Smith Narrative"; McGuire, "Last Hours of Stonewall Jackson."

22 Ibid.

23 Jackson, *Life and Letters*, 471; McGuire, "Last Hours of Stonewall Jackson"; McGuire, "Last Wound of the Late Gen. Jackson," 412. See Appendix I for a detailed discussion of Jackson's final words.

24 Smith, "Lt. Smith Narrative."

25 Ibid.; Alexander Pendleton to father, Sandie Pendleton Papers, VMI.

Chapter Ten

Epilogue

The first indication to those outside Jackson's inner circle that he had died came when a despondent Anna was escorted from the building, supported by her brother Joseph on one side and Jimmy Smith on the other. Witnessing the scene from the main house were Mary Chandler and her 11-year-old daughter, Lucy, who reportedly cried at the time, "O, how willingly I would have died for him."[1]

The new dress coat Jackson was wearing at the time of his wounding had been cut open during his treatment and was not suitable for burial. Instead, Jimmy Smith and Sandie Pendleton dressed Jackson's body in a dark civilian suit and covered that with the general's heavy blue military overcoat. His body was then placed in a simple pine coffin and carried to the parlor of the Chandler home. Viewing the body later that evening, Anna Jackson commented that "all traces of suffering had disappeared from the noble face . . . and he looked more natural than I had dared to hope."[2]

---

1 Lucy Chandler Pendleton to Edward T. Stuart, May 30, 1930; *Herald-Progress* (Ashland, VA), November 25, 1925.

2 Jackson, *Life and Letters*, 472.

Tucker Lacy tried to comfort Anna that Sunday evening by talking to her of Heaven, "giving such glowing descriptions of its blessedness . . . that at last peace, the 'peace of God,' came into my soul," Anna wrote, "and I felt that it was selfish to wish to bring back to this sorrowful earth, for my happiness, one who had made such a blissful exchange. But this frame of mind did not last, and many were the subsequent conflicts to attain and keep this spirit."[3]

After being informed of Jackson's death, Robert E. Lee sent a telegram to Confederate President Jefferson Davis, who stated in reply: "[A] great national calamity has befallen us." The following day, Lee issued General Order No. 61:

> With deep grief, the commanding general announces to the army the death of Lieut. Gen. T. J. Jackson, who expired on the 10th instant, at 3:15 p.m. The daring, skill, and energy of this great and good soldier, by the decree of an all-wise Providence, are now lost to us. But while we mourn his death, we feel that his spirit still lives, and will inspire the whole army with his indomitable courage and unshaken confidence in God as our hope and strength. Let his name be a watchword to his corps, who have followed him to victory on so many fields. Let officers and soldiers emulate his invincible determination to do everything in the defense of our beloved country.
>
> R. E. Lee,
> *General* [4]

In a note that day to Jackson's friend, cavalry general Jeb Stuart, Lee was more personal: "I regret to inform you that the great and good Jackson is no more. He died yesterday at 3:15 p.m., of pneumonia, calm, serene, and happy. May his spirit pervade our whole army; our country will then be secure."[5]

---

3   Ibid., 471-472.

4   *OR* 25, pt. 2, 791, 793.

5   Ibid., 792.

Privately, Lee was heartbroken. That same day he wrote to his wife, "I know not how to replace him," and later openly wept when discussing the death with Sandie Pendleton's father.[6]

On behalf of the officers of the Stonewall Brigade, Lt. Henry K. Douglas approached Lee and asked whether the brigade, or at least part of it, could be allowed to escort the general's remains to Richmond. Keenly aware that his army was constantly outnumbered in battle, Lee sadly denied the request. "I am sure no one can feel the loss of General Jackson more deeply than I do, for no one has the same reasons," Lee said to Douglas. "I am sorry the situation of affairs will not justify me in letting them go to Richmond or even to Lexington. Those people over the river are again showing signs of movement and I cannot leave my headquarters long enough to ride to the depot and pay my dear friend the poor tribute of seeing his body placed upon the cars. He never neglected a duty while living and he would not rest the easier in his grave if his old brigade had left the presence of the enemy to see him buried."[7]

On Monday morning, May 11, Jackson's casket was taken to Guiney Station, where a locomotive and one car were waiting to carry it to Richmond. Upon arriving at the outskirts of the capitol, the train stopped briefly so Anna could detrain and board a waiting carriage, so as to quietly enter the city along more deserted side streets. The train then continued on and pulled into the Richmond station at 4:00 p.m.

The surrounding area was packed with thousands of citizens who had assembled hours earlier in anticipation of seeing the coffin. A deep sorrow "enshrouded every heart," the *Richmond (VA) Enquirer* reported, and "it seemed as if every man felt himself an orphan." The casket was removed from the train, covered with a new flag, and placed on a hearse led by two white horses. Weeks before, the Confederate Congress had authorized the creation of a new national flag, the "Stainless Banner," as it became known due to its large white field. The first flag produced had been assigned to fly

6   Robert E. Lee, *Recollections and Letters of Robert E. Lee* (New York, NY, 1904), 94; Susan Lee, *Memoirs of William Nelson Pendleton*, 274.

7   Douglas, *I Rode with Stonewall*, 228.

Death mask of Jackson made by Frederick Volck.
Valentine Richmond History Center

over the capitol building in Richmond, but it was used instead to drape Jackson's casket.[8]

Every business in Richmond, including government offices, was closed and all flags in the city were flying at half-mast for the arrival of Jackson's body. Major General Arnold Elzey, commander of the Department of Richmond, led a military and civic escort from the train station as church bells throughout the city began to ring, continuing to sound until sundown. Staff members walking behind the hearse included Jimmy Smith, Sandie Pendleton, and Hunter McGuire. With tears streaming down his face, Pendleton would later tell Anna, "God knows I would have died for him."[9]

The long procession slowly made its way to the governor's mansion, where the casket was placed in a reception room. Undertakers embalmed the body later that evening while sculptor Frederick Volck made a death mask of the general's face. The body was then sealed in a new metallic coffin with a glass pane over the face and a silver plate that read: "Lieutenant-General T. J. Jackson. Born January 21st, 1824; died May 10, 1863." The coffin was placed on a bier and surrounded with spring flowers. After viewing the body in state, Anna sadly remarked, "The beloved face could only be seen through the glass plate, which was disappointing and unsatisfactory."[10]

The next morning was very warm. A large funeral procession was organized to take the casket from the executive mansion to the capitol building, where the general's body was to lie in state. The coffin, still draped in the Confederate flag, was placed on a hearse that was now pulled by four white horses. Walking alongside were the pallbearers: Gens. James Longstreet, Richard S. Ewell, Arnold Elzey, George E. Pickett, John H. Winder, Richard B. Garnett, James L. Kemper, Montgomery D. Corse, and George H. Steuart, and Admiral French Forrest of the Confederate navy. Jim

---

8   "Arrival of the Remains of Gen. Thomas J. Jackson," *Richmond (VA) Enquirer*, May 12, 1863.

9   Jackson, *Life and Letters*, 305.

10   "Stonewall Jackson!" *Daily Dispatch* (Richmond, VA), October 26, 1875; Jackson, *Life and Letters*, 474.

Lewis walked behind the hearse leading one of Jackson's horses with reversed boots fastened in the stirrups.[11]

The lengthy procession winding through the streets of Richmond was "very solemn and imposing," one witness described, "because the mourning was sincere and heartfelt." Arriving at the capitol, the pallbearers carried the casket into the House of Representatives' chamber, to which the doors remained open for the public. A reported 20,000 people would file past the casket before the day's end. Henry K. Douglas watched as "a continuous stream" of individuals passed through "for a first and last view of the great general, whom they had learned to honor without seeing and love without knowing." Women brought so many flowers Anna said that "not only the bier was covered, but the table on which it rested overflowed with piles of these numerous tributes of affection."[12]

On Wednesday, May 13, 1863, a military guard escorted the coffin back to the train station, where it departed for Gordonsville en route to Lynchburg, Virginia. "All along the route," Anna recalled, "at every station at which a stop was made, were assembled crowds of people and many were the floral offerings handed in for the bier. His child was often called for, and, on several occasions, was handed in and out of the car windows to be kissed."[13]

Early the next morning in Lynchburg, the casket was placed on the canal boat *Marshall* for a final 15-mile river journey to Lexington, a trip that took a full day. Arriving in the city that evening, the entire corps of cadets of the Virginia Military Institute was waiting at the pier. The coffin was placed on a caisson and taken to Jackson's old classroom at VMI, where it laid in state overnight with an honor guard of cadets.

Although the body had been embalmed in Richmond, the relatively new process had yet to be perfected, and Jackson's body was beginning to show signs of decay. "Decomposition had already taken place," wrote one of the

11 "Funeral Procession in Honor of Lieut. Gen. Thos. J. Jackson," *Daily Dispatch* (Richmond, VA), May 13, 1863; John B. Jones, *A Rebel War Clerk's Diary*, 2 vols. (Philadelphia, PA, 1866), vol.1, 321; Douglas, *I Rode with Stonewall*, 229.

12 Ibid.; Jackson, *Life and Letters*, 475.

13 Ibid., 477.

VMI cadets at Jackson's grave in Lexington, Virginia.
Courtesy of the Virginia Military Institute Archives

honor guards, "in consequence of which his face was not exposed to view as the features were said not to be natural."[14]

On Friday morning at 10:00 a.m., Jackson's military funeral was held at the Presbyterian Church of Lexington, Virginia, in front of an overflowing crowd. Conducting the service was Jackson's pastor, William S. White, who focused his sermon around the 15th chapter of I Corinthians: "The last enemy to be destroyed is death." White finished by tearfully reciting a letter that Jackson had written to the minister after his own son, Capt. Hugh A. White, was killed at the battle of Second Manassas: "The death of your noble son and my much esteemed friend, Hugh, must have been a severe blow to you, yet we have the sweet assurance that, whilst we mourn his loss to the country, to the church, and to ourselves, all has been gain for him. . . . That inconceivable glory to which we are looking forward is already his. . . ."[15]

The two-hour service was followed by another procession that escorted the casket to the Presbyterian cemetery in town, where Stonewall Jackson was buried next to his first daughter with Anna, and not far from his first wife

14 Samuel B. Hannah to unknown correspondent, May 17, 1863, VMI Archives.

15 Lenoir Chambers, *Stonewall Jackson* (New York, NY, 1959), vol. 2, 457.

and stillborn child. Years later, in 1891, Jackson's casket was ceremoniously moved to a nearby vault topped by an eight-foot-tall bronze statue of the general by sculptor Edward V. Valentine. The gravesite and statue remain today in what has been renamed the Stonewall Jackson Memorial Cemetery in Lexington, Virginia.[16]

*   *   *

The Civil War would continue for another two horrific and bloody years after the death of Stonewall Jackson. Some of his friends and comrades would survive the war, others would not. Family members, friends, and artifacts associated with his life took divergent paths following his death:

Mary Anna Jackson

Known throughout the South as "The Widow of the Confederacy," Anna moved to Charlotte, North Carolina, following her husband's death, where she remained active in postwar reunions of Confederate veterans. She never remarried and wore black mourning clothes for the rest of her life. She died at the age of 83 on March 24, 1915, and is buried in Lexington, Virginia, next to her husband.

Julia Laura Jackson Christian

Julia Jackson married William Christian in 1885 and had two children, a daughter named Julia Jackson Christian and a son named Thomas Jonathan Jackson Christian. Her life was cut short at the age of 26 when she contracted typhoid fever and died in 1889. She is buried with her parents in the Stonewall Jackson Memorial Cemetery.

Jim Lewis

Following Jackson's death, Lewis became a servant to Sandie Pendleton until that officer's death in 1864. He then returned to Lexington, Virginia,

---

16 Jackson, *Life and Letters*, 477-478; "Funeral of Lieut. General T. J. Jackson," *Lexington (VA) Gazette*, May 20, 1863; McLaughlin, *Ceremonies Connected with the Unveiling of the Bronze Statue*.

where he died shortly thereafter during the winter of 1864. He is buried in an unmarked grave.

Hunter Holmes McGuire

McGuire remained medical director of the Second Corps for the remainder of the war. Afterward he returned to Richmond, Virginia, where he held the chair of surgery at the Medical College of Virginia. He had a distinguished postwar medical career and was elected president of both the American Surgical Association and the American Medical Association. He suffered a severe stroke in March 1900 and died six months later at the age of 64.

James Power Smith

Smith continued to serve as a general staff officer in the Army of Northern Virginia until the end of the war. He then became minister of the Presbyterian Church of Fredericksburg, Virginia, for 22 years, and was the editor of the *Central Presbyterian* newspaper. He became the oldest surviving member of Jackson's staff, dying in 1923 at the age of 86.

Alexander "Sandie" Pendleton

Rising to the rank of lieutenant colonel, Pendleton was subsequently killed at the battle of Fisher's Hill in September 1864, five days short of his 24th birthday. He is buried in Lexington, Virginia, in the Stonewall Jackson Memorial Cemetery.

Joseph G. Morrison

Jackson's brother-in-law survived the war but lost a foot after suffering a wound at the battle of Petersburg in 1865. He became a cotton mill operator in North Carolina after the war and died at his sister Anna's home in 1906 at the age of 63.

Jedediah Hotchkiss

Hotchkiss continued his duties as a cartographer for the Army of Northern Virginia until the war's end. He moved to Staunton, Virginia, where he had a successful postwar career as an engineer and geologist. He died in 1899 at the age of 70.

Beverly Tucker Lacy

Lacy continued as chaplain to the Second Corps following Jackson's death. He served as pastor for churches in Virginia and Missouri after the war. He died in 1900 at the age of 81, and is buried in the Stonewall Jackson Memorial Cemetery.

Robert E. Lee

Lee remained commander of the Army of Northern Virginia until surrendering his army at Appomattox Court House, Virginia, in April 1865. After the war he served as president of Washington College (now Washington and Lee University) in Lexington, Virginia, until his death in 1870 at the age of 63. He is buried on the university grounds, a short distance from the cemetery containing his trusted lieutenant, Stonewall Jackson.

James Ewell Brown "Jeb" Stuart

Returning to command of the cavalry after the battle of Chancellorsville, Stuart was wounded at the battle of Yellow Tavern on May 11, 1864, and died the next day at the age of 31.

Ambrose Powell "A. P." Hill

Surviving his wound at the battle of Chancellorsville, Hill was promoted to corps command following Jackson's death. He would be killed in action at the age of 39 during the battle of Petersburg in April 1865.

Little Sorrel

Immediately after Jackson's wounding, his favorite war horse was caught by two men from Capt. Marcellus Moorman's artillery battery. Not realizing at the time the horse was Jackson's, one of the soldiers rode him for several days until someone recognized Little Sorrel. The horse was turned in to Moorman, who subsequently turned the animal over to Gen. Jeb Stuart.

Little Sorrel on the parade grounds at VMI.
Courtesy of the Virginia Military Institute Archives

Little Sorrel was then given to Anna Jackson, who took the horse with her to live at her father's house near Charlotte, North Carolina, where "he was treated to the greenest of pastures and the best of care."[17]

While in North Carolina, Little Sorrel developed the unique ability to lift latches with his mouth, and routinely used the skill to let himself out of his stall. The "old rascal," Anna recalled, would then "go deliberately to the doors of all the other horses and mules, liberate each one, and then march off with them all behind him, like a soldier leading his command, to the green fields of grain around the farm."[18]

In 1883, her father having advanced in age and finding it more difficult to care for the animal, Anna donated Little Sorrel to the Virginia Military Institute, where the horse leisurely grazed the parade grounds for the next

17 Marcellus Moorman to Thomas J. Jackson, May 10, 1863, Dabney-Jackson Collection, box 1, LVA; Newspaper clippings, February 2, 1885 and February 16, 1885, Hotchkiss Collection, reel 58, LC; Jackson, *Life and Letters*, 171-172.

18 Ibid.

Little Sorrel's preserved hide at the VMI Museum.
VMI Museum, Lexington, Virginia

two years. Following a brief stint in an exhibition at the 1885 World's Fair in New Orleans, Little Sorrel was relocated to the Confederate Soldiers' Home in Richmond, Virginia, where he died in 1886 at the age of 36.[19]

The Soldiers' Home had previously arranged for Washington, D.C. taxidermist Frederic S. Webster to preserve Little Sorrel's hide upon the animal's death. Webster traveled to Richmond and removed the horse's hide

19 Newspaper clippings, February 2, 1885 and February 16, 1885, Hotchkiss Collection, reel 58, LC; "Stonewall Jackson's War Horse," *New York Times*, November 27, 1887; *Boston Daily Globe*, January 29, 1885.

from its skeleton, explaining that "the skin of any large animal is likely to deteriorate, if the bones and ligaments are used when mounting the specimen." He then mounted the hide over a framework of plaster. Webster kept the skeletal remains "as part payment for my service."[20]

Little Sorrel's mounted hide found its way back to Lexington, Virginia, in 1949 where it remains on display in the VMI Museum. Frederic Webster kept the skeleton and took it with him to the Carnegie Museum in Pittsburgh, Pennsylvania, when he became chief curator of the institution in 1897. The museum donated the skeleton to VMI in 1949, where it remained in storage until 1997. The bones were then cremated and buried on the VMI parade grounds at the foot of the statue of Stonewall Jackson.

Jackson's Raincoat

The oil-cloth raincoat Stonewall Jackson was wearing at the time of his wounding was cut open along the front of the left sleeve and across the chest before being removed and left on the battlefield. The coat was found a few days later by a hungry scavenger who sold the coat for a gallon of meal to the overseer of the nearby Ellwood estate. The overseer's wife repaired the coat several months later by sewing up the split left sleeve and patching the bullet holes. The coat was sold, reportedly for $125, in November 1864 to Joseph Bryan, a wounded soldier on furlough.[21]

Bryan discovered "T. J. Jackson" written in the back of the coat and instantly realized its significance. He wore the coat only sparingly until 1867, when his father forwarded it to Robert E. Lee, then president of Washington College, asking him to determine who should rightfully possess it. In a letter to the elder Bryan acknowledging receipt, Lee thanked him for sending "me so interesting a relic of one whose memory is so dear to me." He thought it was best to first consult with Anna Jackson, "whose wishes on the subject are entitled to consideration."[22]

20 Frederic S. Webster, letter excerpts, July 15, 1939, VMI Museum.

21 "Sold for a Gallon of Meal," *The Free-Lance* (Fredericksburg, VA), July 28, 1891; Anonymous, "Oil-Cloth Coat in which Jackson Received His Mortal Wound," in *SHSP* (January 1891), vol. 19, 324-326.

22 R. E. Lee to J. R. Bryan, December 13, 1867, VHS.

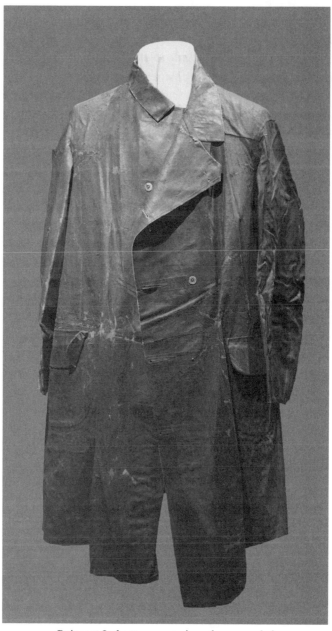

Raincoat Jackson was wearing when wounded.
VMI Museum, Lexington, Virginia

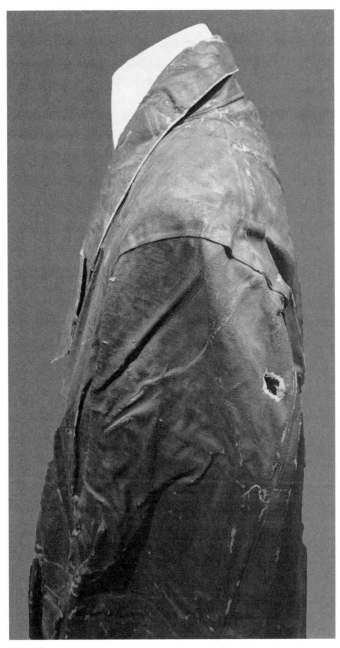

Side view of raincoat with bullet hole visible in left shoulder.
VMI Museum, Lexington, Virginia

Anna answered an inquiry from Lee in January 1868, writing: "Such a relic of my precious martyred husband would be extremely painful to me, and yet I cannot reconcile myself to think of its being in any other possession than my own." Forwarding the coat to Anna, Lee responded, "It has appeared to me most proper that this relic of your husband, though painfully recalling his death, should be possessed by you. It is a familiar object to my sight, and must recall sad reminiscences to the mind of every soldier of the Army of N.Va."[23]

Anna kept the coat until later that year, when she gave it to the Reverend David Macrae, a visiting minister from Scotland. Admiring the coat after seeing it at her house, Macrae asked Mrs. Jackson whether he could take it home with him for others to view. She would later recall in a letter to Hunter McGuire how the minister "begged me very hard for it," and since it was "such a painful relic" for her, she did not desire to keep it. Returning to Dundee, Scotland, Macrae had the coat placed on display in a museum, where it quietly remained for the next 30 years.[24]

Macrae returned to the United States in 1899, during which time Hunter McGuire and his wife urged Anna Jackson to ask the minister to return the coat so it could be displayed in the Confederate Museum in Richmond. Macrae did visit with Anna, but refused her request to return the coat on the grounds that the Confederate Museum already had "numberless and valuable relics" pertaining to Jackson, and hoped that she would "not grudge that one relic to the land that Jackson himself loved so well, and where perhaps as many even of the Americans can see it as they would in Richmond, for numberless Americans visit Scotland every year."[25]

For some unknown reason, Macrae had a change of heart upon returning to Scotland; he finally sent the coat back to Anna Jackson. This time she refused to entrust the coat to anyone, including the museum, and it remained in her possession until she passed away in 1915. After her death, the raincoat was passed down to her granddaughter, Julia Jackson Christian Preston, who donated it to the Virginia Military Institute. The coat, with a bullet hole still

23 R. E. Lee to J. R. Bryan, January 18, 1868, VHS; R. E. Lee to M. A. Jackson, January 18, 1868, Lee Family Papers, VHS.

24 M. A. Jackson to Dr. McGuire, February 7, 1899, VHS.

25 M. A. Jackson to Dr. McGuire, February 7, 1899, VHS; Hunter McGuire to Mrs. Joseph Bryan, February 8, 1899, VHS; David Macrae to Mrs. McGuire, February 2, 1899, VHS.

visible in the upper left sleeve, remains on display in the VMI museum a few steps away from Little Sorrel.[26]

---

26 David F. Riggs, "Stonewall Jackson's Raincoat," in *Civil War Times Illustrated* (July 1977), vol. 16, 37-41.

Appendix I

Controversies Surrounding the Event

The he story of Stonewall Jackson's wounding and death involves several elements that have been the focus of discussion and controversy from 1863 through the present day. While the definitive answer to many of these questions may never be determined, the following interpretations are based on the currently available historical evidence.

Plank Road or Mountain Road

Recent interpretations of the circumstances surrounding Stonewall Jackson's wounding have maintained that Jackson and his staff reconnoitered down the small, isolated Mountain Road running parallel to the Plank Road and that he received his wounds while on this path. This interpretation is supported by one eyewitness account, that of Pvt. David Kyle, who claimed to have been guiding Jackson at the time. Kyle's account, which contradicts all other eyewitness accounts, has been given credence on the basis that he was a local youth who would be more knowledgeable of the surrounding geography. To accept this interpretation, one must also accept that all of the other individuals involved in the event had—in the bright moonlight—mistaken the isolated, narrow, dirt pathway of the Mountain Road to be the wide, wood-planked, main Orange Plank Road they believed they were on.[1]

For 30 years following the wounding, no open controversy existed as to which road Jackson had taken on the night of May 2, 1863. Then in the early 1890s, Augustus Choate Hamlin began research for his book *The Battle of Chancellorsville: The Attack of Stonewall Jackson and his Army, Upon the Right Flank of the Army of the Potomac, 1863.* Hamlin interviewed and corresponded with numerous Union and Confederate veterans in addition to visiting the battlefield. On one of those visits, Hamlin was introduced to James Talley and J. Horace Lacy, two local landowners who insisted well after the war that Jackson had ridden down the Mountain Road, where he was actually shot by Union soldiers. Since neither Talley nor Lacy were present at the time of the wounding, they backed their story up by introducing Hamlin to Kyle, the local boy who claimed to have led Jackson down the Mountain Road.

Hamlin attempted to confirm Kyle's story by corresponding with several Confederate officers present at Chancellorsville. Both William Palmer, of A. P. Hill's staff, and Joseph Morrison disputed the Mountain Road location. In a letter to Hamlin in 1894, Palmer wrote: "You will see that Capt. Leigh and Capt. Wilbourn exactly agree, as to where we were when first fired on, from the right or south side of the Pike. There are three witnesses to this point and the location of the dismantled house on the right, or south side makes it very certain to me that we are correct and Kyle 9th Virginia Cavalry, wrong, as to this point."[2]

Brigadier General James H. Lane, whose North Carolina regiment accidentally shot Jackson, sent at least three letters to Hamlin rejecting the claim that Jackson was on the Mountain Road, vehemently writing in 1892, "As I have said in my last, I have never since that night seen nor heard anything to change my opinion as to when, how, and where Jackson was

---

1   Robert K. Krick, *The Smoothbore Volley that Doomed the Confederacy* (Baton Rouge, LA, 2002).

2   Joseph G. Morrison to A. C. Hamlin, May 3, 1895, ACHC, Harvard University; Extracts of Joseph G. Morrison letter to G. W. Sanderlin, 1895, ACHC, Harvard University; William Palmer to A. C. Hamlin, September 15, 1894, ACHC, Harvard University.

Detail of Hotchkiss map indicating location of Jackson's wounding.
Library of Congress

wounded." Nevertheless, when Hamlin published his book in 1896, he described Kyle leading Jackson and his staff down the Mountain Road.[3]

Kyle then sent a manuscript describing details of the event to the *Confederate Veteran* magazine. His edited account was published in 1896 and an unedited version of the letter exists at the Fredericksburg and Spotsylvania National Military Park.[4]

Publication of both Kyle's account and Hamlin's book sparked another round of rebuttal among Jackson's staff. In letters between Jedediah Hotchkiss and James P. Smith, both rejected the Mountain Road as the location of the reconnaissance and the wounding. When G. F. R. Henderson contacted Hotchkiss for help with his book *Stonewall Jackson and the American Civil War*, published in 1898, the cartographer commented on the recent controversy. "The whole matter was talked over among the staff and no one ever spoke of Jackson's having been on any road but the direct one to Chancellorsville until recently." He went on to warn Henderson: "If you

3   James H. Lane to A. C. Hamlin, November 30, 1892, September 30, 1892, November 17, 1892, January 5, 1895, ACHC, Harvard University; Hamlin, *The Battle of Chancellorsville*, 108-109.

4   Kyle, "Jackson's Guide When Shot"; Kyle, manuscript for *CV* magazine (1895).

follow Hamlin's statements you will make great mistakes. He is laboring to establish a theory and to twist everything to agree with that theory."[5]

A close examination of Kyle's account raises questions as to its accuracy. Kyle states that while on the Mountain Road, Jackson started to leave the path and "turned his horse head toward the south . . . just as his horses front feet had cleared the edge of the road whilste his hind feet was still on the edge of the bank," Jackson was shot. After the volley, Kyle states that Little Sorrel "wheeled to the right and started to run." Kyle then goes on to describe in detail Jackson's removal from the field—an ordeal during which Kyle curiously remains a detached bystander watching from horseback, never helping to remove Jackson from his horse, carry the litter, search for a surgeon, or lend aid in any way.[6]

Kyle's statement that Jackson was facing south at the time of the shooting would place the 18th North Carolina Regiment to Jackson's right. It would be impossible in such a position for Jackson to be shot in the left arm, as his body would have shielded that extremity from the fire. In addition, if Little Sorrel "wheeled to the right" from that position, the horse would have turned into and run toward the musket fire, an unlikely reaction from a frightened animal. For the event to occur as Kyle describes, the volley that wounded Jackson would have had to come from the Union side—the story Talley and Lacy were trying to sell Hamlin.

Using trajectory analysis, Jackson's left side would have to be facing the 18th North Carolina in order for him to receive the wounds as detailed by McGuire. Jackson's bridle hand was his left, and the wound in that forearm was described as follows: "a ball having entered the outside of the forearm, an inch below the elbow, came out upon the opposite side just above the wrist." For Jackson to be wounded by the 18th North Carolina with a bullet taking that path through the arm, he could not have been directly facing the regiment, nor could he have been facing south.

It is reasonable to assume that McGuire's description of the bullet path was accurate, since it is unlikely that an experienced Civil War surgeon would have misidentified entrance and exit wounds, the appearances of

5   James P. Smith to Jedediah Hotchkiss, July 21, 1897, Hotchkiss Papers, reel 14, LC; Jedediah Hotchkiss to James P. Smith, July 23, 1897, Hotchkiss Papers, reel 34, LC; Jedediah Hotchkiss to G. F. R. Henderson, July 23, 1897, Hotchkiss Papers, reel 34, LC.

6   Kyle, manuscript for *CV* magazine (1895).

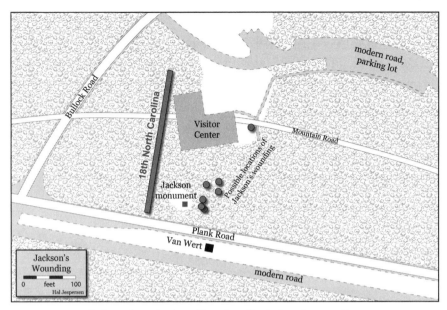

Independent plotting of locations for Jackson's wounding
as specified in primary accounts.

which were well known and described by military surgery texts of the period. In *A Manual of Military Surgery for use of Surgeons in the Confederate Army*, J. Julian Chisolm writes: "Balls, whether round or elongated, usually make an irregularly rounded entrance, surrounded by discoloration, depressed, inverted tissues—these having been evidently mashed or crushed by the ball prior to its entrance, and the skin drawn in to a certain extent with it. The tissues around the orifice of exit are lacerated, usually more less protruding, and the orifice probably larger, and more irregular than where the ball entered."[7]

Bullet trajectory instead supports Richard E. Wilbourn's account, in which he describes that the group, on returning from the front, left the Plank Road and entered the woods to the right, with Jackson "approaching our lines diagonally" when he was shot. This positioning would place Jackson's left arm, and more importantly his left elbow, directly in the line of fire from the 18th North Carolina. Further accounts by Wilbourn, along with those by Smith, Morrison, and period newspaper articles, all place the location of

7   Chisolm, *A Manual of Military Surgery*, 159.

Jackson's wounding in the woods a short distance north of the Plank Road. For Jackson to receive his left arm wounds by the initial volley of the Confederate line, he had to be riding through the woods and toward—not on—the Mountain Road at the time.[8]

The presence of all participants and witnesses to Jackson's wounding can be confirmed in the narratives of others—except that of David Kyle. None of the surviving first-person accounts mention Kyle as being present. For Kyle to have played such an important role in the event and yet escape mention by others seems unlikely. As a result, both his presence and his story are unsupported by the surviving evidence. The staff members of Jackson and A. P. Hill who were present at Chancellorsville and who documented the reconnaissance as occurring down the Plank Road are substantial and convincing: Richard Wilbourn, James Smith, Joseph Morrison, William Palmer, William Randolph, Marcellus Moorman, Benjamin Leigh, James Lane, Hunter McGuire, and Jed Hotchkiss. Since acceptance of Kyle's singular account requires rejection of all the others, the overwhelming evidence supports the theory that Jackson reconnoitered down the Plank Road, entered the woods north of the road while returning to his lines, and received his wounds in a location between the Plank and Mountain Roads.

Number of Falls from the Litter

Another controversy surrounding Jackson's wounding concerns the number of times Jackson fell from the litter during his removal from the battlefield. Several modern accounts of the event relate two falls: one when a litter bearer was wounded, and a second when another bearer tripped on a vine while walking in the woods. However, every first-person account of the event—save one—describes only a single fall as having occurred. The lone exception came in a letter written by Joseph Morrison in 1879. The

---

8 McGuire, "Last Wound of the Late Gen. Jackson," 406; Richard E. Wilbourn to Robert Dabney, December 12, 1863; Richard E. Wilbourn to Charles Faulkner, May 1863; Richard E. Wilbourn to Jubal A. Early, February 19, 1873; James P. Smith to Mr. Stuart, April 27, 1905, Thomas J. Jackson Collection, MOC; Joseph G. Morrison to Spier Whitaker, June 27, 1900, VHS; "The Death of Stonewall Jackson," *Daily Richmond Whig*, October 7, 1865; Edward E. Hueske, *Practical Analysis and Reconstruction of Shooting Incidents* (Boca Raton, FL, 2006).

confusion seems to arise from the fact that some accounts document the fall as occurring after the bearer was wounded, while others mention it only when a bearer trips in the woods.

An 1878 article in the *Southern Historical Society Papers* written by Jubal A. Early, one of Jackson's divisional generals who was not present during the event, appears to be the first narrative that describes Jackson as suffering two separate falls from the litter. Early's primary source for the article was Capt. Richard Wilbourn, who wrote a series of letters to Early in which he described Jackson falling from the stretcher only once, as a result of a litter bearer being wounded. In order to continue the story after the point at which Wilbourn wrote that he left the scene, Early turned to previous accounts written by Benjamin Leigh and James Smith. Both authors described a single fall from the litter during Jackson's removal, but document it as happening when a litter bearer tripped in the woods. Since Leigh and Smith related a fall under different circumstances than the one by Wilbourn, Early combined the accounts into a single narrative detailing two separate falls from the litter.[9]

Combining the accounts in such a fashion is problematic, as Wilbourn actually changed details of his story over time. The earliest known account describing Jackson's wounding is a letter Wilbourn wrote within days of the event—prior even to Jackson's death—to Lt. Col. Charles Faulkner, the Second Corps assistant adjutant general. In that letter, Wilbourn specifically mentions that "one of the litter bearers had his arm broken but did not let the litter fall—then another man just after this fell with the litter, in consequence of getting his foot tangled in a vine." Wilbourn's subsequent accounts and letters, including the one he sent to Early, alter the story to Jackson falling when the bearer was wounded, and he completely omits any reference to another bearer tripping in the woods.[10]

Following the publication of Early's article, Joseph Morrison wrote a letter to the author disagreeing with some minor details. Morrison's letter notes that Jackson fell "about 3 feet" from the litter when the bearer was

---

9 Early, "Stonewall Jackson—The Story of His Being an Astrologer Refuted—An Eyewitness Describes How He Was Wounded," 261-282; Richard E. Wilbourn to Jubal A. Early, February 18, 1873; Richard E. Wilbourn to Jubal A. Early, February 19, 1873; Richard E. Wilbourn to Jubal A. Early, March 3, 1873.

10 Richard E. Wilbourn to Charles Faulkner, May 1863.

wounded and a second fall occurred when a bearer tripped "tho this time the fall was very light." Prior to Morrison's letter, all first-person accounts, including one Morrison wrote himself in 1866 for the magazine *The Land We Love*, described only a single fall from the litter.[11]

Benjamin W. Leigh of A. P. Hill's staff wrote a letter to his wife on May 12, 1863, detailing circumstances of the event. In his letter, Leigh states they were compelled to lay Jackson down in the middle of the road during the artillery barrage that wounded the bearer, and later one of the "litter bearers got his foot tangled in a grapevine and fell—letting Gen. Jackson fall on his broken arm."[12]

James P. Smith, who was carrying the corner of the litter opposite that of the wounded bearer, consistently maintained in all accounts that Leigh caught the corner of litter when the bearer was wounded, preventing Jackson from falling, and that the general rolled off only when another bearer tripped in the woods. Jackson himself, in relating details of the event to others, as recorded by Hunter McGuire and Tucker Lacy, spoke repeatedly of his "fall" from the litter—singular, not plural.[13]

As the story of Jackson's wounding was told and retold by eyewitnesses for decades after the actual event, details blurred and facts merged to cause confusion and disagreement in written accounts. If one ascribes to the idea that the most accurate reports are likely to be those written within the shortest time following the actual event, when memories are the most fresh, then Wilbourn's original account to Faulkner and Leigh's letter to his wife would be deemed the most factual. Both accounts, written within days of the event by individuals on different staffs, corroborate each other perfectly in documenting that Jackson suffered only one fall from the stretcher and that it occurred after a litter bearer tripped on a vine in the woods. The multiple, consistent narratives from Smith—who was a litter bearer at the time—serve as confirmatory evidence of this single-fall interpretation.

11 Joseph G. Morrison to Jubal A. Early, February 20, 1878, Jubal Anderson Early Papers, vol. 10, LC; [Morrison], "Wounding of Lieutenant-General T. J. Jackson."

12 Benjamin W. Leigh to wife, May 12, 1863.

13 James P. Smith to Jedediah Hotchkiss, n.d.; Smith, "Lt. Smith Narrative"; Smith, "Stonewall Jackson's Last Battle"; McGuire, "Last Hours of Stonewall Jackson"; Lacy, "Narrative."

Last Words

Perhaps the best-known aspect of Jackson's death is the uttering of his final words: "Let us cross over the river and rest under the shade of the trees." Despite several primary sources documenting that Jackson spoke the words, in the years following Jackson's death some questions were raised as to the authenticity of the quote.

Initial confusion concerning the phrase centered on its exact wording, as some accounts quote the verb "pass" in place of "cross." For instance, the two most widely read early biographies of Jackson use different quotes. John Esten Cooke, in his 1866 book *Stonewall Jackson: A Military Biography*, uses the words "cross over the river," while Robert L. Dabney writes "pass over the river" in his 1866 *Life and Campaigns of Lieut-Gen. Thomas J. Jackson*. Anna Jackson was the likely source for Dabney's book, as her personal account to him uses "pass" in the phrase she records as being her husband's "last audible words." However, in her two postwar books, *Life and Letters of General Thomas J. Jackson* (1891) and *Memoirs of Stonewall Jackson* (1895), Anna uses the phrase "cross over the river."[14]

It was the publication of *Life and Letters* that led to the most noted questioning of the event. In the margin of his copy of the book, Henry K. Douglas, one of Jackson's assistant adjutants at the time, wrote next to the quote: "I never believed Jackson said that and don't believe it now." A later, undated addition to the margin by Douglas read, "When I doubted—after the war, I wrote to Smith of Richmond that he heard the General speak the words. I never believed it until he . . . told me that he heard it." Douglas was convinced enough to eventually use the phrase as Jackson's last words in his own manuscript, *I Rode with Stonewall* (1899).[15]

The most widely cited descriptions of Jackson's deathbed scene, including his last words, are from his doctor, Hunter H. McGuire, and were published in *The Richmond Medical Journal* (1866) and the *Southern Historical Society Papers* (1886). Although McGuire's accounts have

---

14 Cooke, *Stonewall Jackson: A Military Biography*, 444; Dabney, *Life and Campaigns*, 711; Jackson, "Narrative"; Jackson, *Life and Letters*, 471; Anna Jackson, *Memoirs of Stonewall Jackson by his Widow Mary Anna Jackson* (Louisville, KY, 1895), 457.

15 A copy of the marginalia is in bound volume 176, FSNMP; Douglas, *I Rode With Stonewall*, 228.

become the accepted version of Jackson's final moments, the physician admits in an early handwritten account to his friend Jed Hotchkiss that he was not present when Jackson said his final words. In the letter, McGuire writes that he left the room and "those who remained report that a smile of ineffable sweetness spread itself over his pale face and he added presently, 'Let us cross over the river and rest under the shade of the trees,' and then without pain or the least struggle he died." McGuire omitted from his later accounts the fact that he was not in the room at the exact moment of Jackson's death and during the speaking of the famous phrase.[16]

Any question of Jackson's final words being a postwar fabrication is dispelled by the fact that the quote was widely circulated in newspapers within days of his death. Both the Richmond *Sentinel* on May 16, 1863, and the Richmond *Daily Dispatch* on May 20, 1863, quote an earlier story from the *Central Presbyterian* that record Jackson's final words as being: "Let us cross over the river and rest under the shade of the trees."

The timing of the phrase, however, is more ambiguous. Most postwar accounts dramatize the scene by giving the impression that Jackson uttered the words immediately prior to his death. In her account of the event for Dabney's book, Anna Jackson states that her husband said the words while in a "dozing state" and they were his "last <u>audible</u> words" (underline present in original manuscript). McGuire, who left the room "about half an hour before he died," admits to not hearing the words before leaving. Jimmy Smith, who apparently entered before McGuire left, did hear the phrase, but related to Dabney that Jackson spoke no more after approximately 2:30 p.m. Taking the accounts together, with allowances for inexact timing due to recall, it appears that Jackson spoke the phrase 30 to 45 minutes before he died at 3:15 p.m.[17]

Although the romanticized version, with Jackson uttering the phrase with his last dying breath, is not supported by the primary accounts of those in the room at the time, there is sufficient evidence to document they were his last intelligible words and that he uttered them approximately 30 minutes before he died.

16 McGuire, "Last Wound of the Late Gen. Jackson," 412; McGuire, "Death of Stonewall Jackson," 162; McGuire, "Last Hours of Stonewall Jackson."

17 Jackson, "Narrative"; McGuire, "Last Hours of Stonewall Jackson"; Smith, "Narrative."

Cause of Death

Hunter H. McGuire and the other military physicians involved in Jackson's care established pneumonia as the immediate cause of his death. That diagnosis was largely unquestioned until more modern times, when medical authorities reviewed the case and offered alternate possibilities. Most of the newly suggested diagnoses center around blood clots to the lungs (pulmonary embolus) or septicemia, also known as blood poisoning. Although medical knowledge at the time of the Civil War was limited in regard to both the causes and treatment of most diseases, physicians of the time were able to differentiate many conditions based on their presentation and physical findings.[18]

Medical statistics of the Civil War reveal that "inflammation of the lungs and pleura," the classification to which pneumonia belonged, was the third most common cause of death from disease during the conflict. Pneumonia was an easily recognized and frequently encountered condition that carried a 24 percent mortality rate in the pre-antibiotic era of the Civil War. In describing pneumonia, a respected medical textbook of the era stated that the diagnosis of "no disease is more readily recognized in a large majority of cases," and that it was "the most fatal of all acute diseases." Without means to alter the course of pneumonia, 19th-century physicians were able to observe the natural history of the disease and became adept at predicting its outcome. Hunter McGuire demonstrated this remarkable ability when he informed Anna Jackson on May 10, 1863, that her husband had but two

---

18 L. Whittington Gorham, "What Was the Cause of Stonewall Jackson's Death?" *Archives of Internal Medicine* (1963), vol. 111, 52-56; Joe D. Haines, "What Killed Stonewall Jackson," *Journal of the Oklahoma State Medical Association* (1998), vol. 91, 162-165; Timothy R. Koch and Joseph B. Kirsner, "Chronic Gastrointestinal Symptoms of Thomas 'Stonewall' Jackson following Mexican-American War Exposure: A Medical Hypothesis," *Military Medicine* (2007), vol. 172, 6-8; Marvin P. Rozear and Joseph C. Greenfield, "'Let Us Cross Over the River': The Final Illness of Stonewall Jackson," *Virginia Magazine of History and Biography* (1995), vol. 103, 29-46; Alan D. Smith, "Stonewall Jackson and His Surgeon, Hunter McGuire," *Bulletin of the N.Y. Academy of Medicine* (1973), vol. 49, 594-609; Beverly C. Smith, "The Last Illness and Death of General Thomas Jonathan (Stonewall) Jackson," *Virginia Military Institute Alumni Review* (1975), vol. 51, 8-13.

hours to live, then pronouncing Jackson dead one hour and forty-five minutes later.[19]

Patients dying from pneumonia typically progressed through stages of prostration, "muttering delirium," drowsiness, semi-consciousness, and coma—all consistent with Jackson's course of illness. Succumbing to pneumonia was such a peaceful way of passing in the 19th century that the disease was euphemistically referred to as "the old man's friend."[20]

With such a familiarity with pneumonia and its presentation, it is highly improbable that all five physicians involved in Jackson's care at Guiney Station would misdiagnose another disease as pneumonia. As a result, Jackson almost assuredly had the condition, and the course of his illness and death is consistent with the natural history of pneumonia before outcomes were altered by the present-day use of antibiotics.

McGuire and the other military physicians attributed the development of Jackson's pneumonia to a lung bruise, or pulmonary contusion, that he may have suffered after his fall from the litter. Pulmonary contusions during the Civil War often occurred—as they do today—without any evidence of external injury or rib fracture. In modern medicine, early-onset pneumonia (occurring within three to four days of injury) continues to be a well-recognized complication of pulmonary contusions.[21]

As the germ theory of disease had not yet been advanced at the time of the Civil War, physicians had no knowledge of bacteria, and consequently no understanding of the need for sterile technique. Nonetheless, Civil War surgeons recognized septicemia—or pyemia, as it was often called at the time—as an almost uniformly fatal complication that could occur after amputation. With no knowledge of bacteria being the cause, physicians of the time classified septicemia as a condition resulting solely from an infected wound site. Much like pneumonia, septicemia following amputation had a specific presentation that was familiar to military surgeons.

19 Smart, *The Medical and Surgical History of the War of the Rebellion* (Washington, D.C., 1888), pt. 3, vol. 1, 751-810; William Osler, *The Principles and Practice of Medicine*, 3rd ed. (New York, NY, 1898), 132.

20 Mathew W. Lively, "Stonewall Jackson and the Old Man's Friend," *Journal of Medical Biography* (2011), vol. 19, 84-88.

21 Mathew W. Lively, "Early Onset Pneumonia Following Pulmonary Contusion: The Case of Stonewall Jackson," *Military Medicine* (2012), vol. 177, 315-317.

Pyemia at the time was almost uniformly fatal and typically presented with the onset of severe chills and sweats, followed by a jaundiced, or yellowed, appearance of the skin. A period of "tranquility," in which the patient seemed improved, often occurred after the onset of the illness, followed by a recurrence of fever and chills. Since septicemia during the Civil War was attributed to an infected wound, the disease was often described as being associated with changes at the surgical site. Initially an abundance of pus would flow from the wound, but as the disease progressed the discharge would become thin, watery, and foul smelling, followed by sloughing and separation of the closed incision.[22]

As he first mentioned in his 1866 article for the *Richmond Medical Journal*, McGuire wrote descriptions of Jackson's well-healing operative site religiously to document that Jackson showed none of the typical signs of pyemia as recognized at the time.[23]

Today, modern medical science understands that septicemia is the systemic response to the presence of pathologic microorganisms in the bloodstream, and that the condition can result from a multitude of sources other than simply an infected wound. Pathologically speaking, Stonewall Jackson did have septicemia. But in medical and legal terms, "cause of death" is defined as "the disease or injury that initiated the train of events leading to death." In other words, without that underlying cause, death would not have resulted. For Jackson, the disease that initiated his death was either pneumonia or a wound infection.[24]

When the available evidence from primary sources is analyzed, Jackson's illness, or underlying cause of death, is most consistent with the diagnosis of pneumonia. It is this disease that likely initiated the train of events leading to sepsis and eventual death.

---

22 Chisolm, *Manual of Military Surgery*, 248-249; William W. Keen, "Surgical Reminiscences of the Civil War," in *Addresses and Other Papers* (Philadelphia, PA, 1905), 430-431.

23 McGuire, "Last Wound of the Late Gen. Jackson," 1866.

24 Walter E. Finkbeiner, Philip C. Ursell, and Richard L. Davis, *Autopsy Pathology: A Manual and Atlas*, 2nd ed. (Philadelphia, PA, 2009), 151.

Jackson's Arm

Following the amputation of Stonewall Jackson's left arm on May 3, 1863, Rev. Beverly Tucker Lacy found the extremity "wrapped up outside (the) tent." According to Lacy's account of the incident given to Robert Dabney for his book *Life and Campaigns of Lieut-Gen. Thomas J. Jackson*, the pastor buried it "in a private graveyard of J. H. Lacy." The Ellwood estate owned by Tucker Lacy's brother, J. Horace Lacy, was located one mile from the Second Corps Field Hospital. A family cemetery is situated 300 yards from the Ellwood house, and Tucker Lacy buried Jackson's arm somewhere within that graveyard. He does not specify in his account the exact location of the burial nor whether he marked the spot in some fashion. Jedediah Hotchkiss wrote in his journal on May 3, 1863, that he buried his friend James Keith Boswell in the same cemetery "by the side of General Jackson's arm which had been amputated and buried there."[25]

The battle of the Wilderness was fought in same area one year later, with Ellwood serving as a headquarters for the Union army. Colonel Charles E. Phelps of the 7th Maryland made an interesting entry in his diary on May 6, 1864: "left in front behind Arty. 200 yds from here where S. Jackson died. His arm dug up by some pioneers + re-buried." How the soldiers knew the location of the arm is unknown; also unspecified is whether or not they placed the arm back in its original site.[26]

Union engineer Wesley Brainerd records in his memoirs that the following day he also visited the location, but that it was "unmarked by stone or board." Although he describes "the little mound of earth before me," he mistakenly believed Jackson's entire body was buried there, as the dirt "hid from view all that was mortal of the man whose great deeds had filled the world with wonder and amazement."[27]

Following the Civil War, James Power Smith, Jackson's former aide-de-camp, married the daughter of J. Horace Lacy and worked as pastor of the Presbyterian Church in Fredericksburg. In 1903—40 years after the arm was buried—Smith placed a stone marker in the family cemetery

---

25 Lacy, "Narrative"; Hotchkiss, *Make Me a Map of the Valley*, 140.

26 Diary of Charles E. Phelps, from a transcript located at FSNMP.

27 Malles, ed., *Bridge Building in Wartime*, 213.

Present-day photograph of marker for Jackson's arm placed by James P. Smith in 1903.
Author's photo

inscribed with the words: "Arm of Stonewall Jackson, May 3, 1863." Based on his closeness to the situation, friendship with Tucker Lacy, and status as the son-in-law of the estate's owner, Smith likely had direct knowledge of the arm's location, but he may not have placed the marker directly over the spot. He may have deliberately placed the stone away from the location in an effort to prevent further desecration, as committed by Union soldiers after the battle of the Wilderness. Equally plausible, he may have placed the stone merely as a tribute to the event and not as a grave marker, an action that would be consistent with the other nine markers he placed around the battlefield, all of which are in approximate locations.

The other well-known event surrounding Jackson's arm concerns Brig. Gen. Smedley Butler and the U.S. Marine Corps. From September 26 – October 5, 1921, the Marine East Coast Expeditionary Force from Quantico, Virginia, completed maneuvers on the Wilderness battlefield. According to family tradition recounted by the grandson of the owner of Ellwood at the time, Butler expressed disbelief when told that Jackson's arm was buried on site. To verify the claim, the general allegedly had a squad of soldiers dig at the spot of the Smith marker. After finding the arm bone in a box a few feet below the surface, Butler reportedly had the relic placed in a metal box and reburied in the same spot. The Marines then had a commemorative plaque made and affixed to the stone.

The Marine Corps maneuvers were well publicized at the time and several major newspapers covered the event in a series of articles. Neither the newspaper articles nor official reports of the event document Butler having the arm exhumed and reburied. The *New York Times* of October 3, 1921, does detail a visit by then-President Warren G. Harding to the cemetery following a review of the troops at Ellwood. The article goes on to describe the graveyard as being "overgrown with weeds" when the Marines first arrived and that they "asked permission of the owner of the farm on which the cemetery is situated to put it in condition in honor of Jackson." By the time of Harding's visit, the soldiers had erected a "neat fence of white posts and wire around the five big cedar trees that rise above the unmarked graves and the stone marking where Jackson's arm lies."[28]

If Butler's men had actually exhumed Jackson's arm and reburied it in a metal box, it is doubtful that such a momentous event would have escaped mention in the newspapers. Instead, the Expeditionary Force likely placed the plaque on the stone simply as their own tribute to Jackson and not to commemorate a reburial of the arm bone.

In 1998, the National Park Service decided to open Ellwood to the public, but feared publicity surrounding the location of Jackson's arm could tempt looters to dig at the site. The agency decided to protect the artifact by first locating its exact location, followed by the pouring of a concrete apron over it. Despite an extensive archeological survey, the Park Service failed to discover a metal box, and found no evidence that a grave shaft had ever been dug near the stone marker. The Service's final conclusion was that the Smedley Butler story was probably fictional and that Jackson's arm remains buried within the cemetery in an unknown and unmarked location.

---

28 John H. Craige, "The Wilderness Maneuvers," *Marine Corps Gazette* (December 1921), vol. 6, 418-423; "President Praises Men of the Marines," *New York Times*, October 3, 1921.

Appendix II

Building the Stonewall Image

Prior to the battle of First Manassas in July 1861, Thomas J. Jackson was a relatively obscure instructor at the Virginia Military Institute in Lexington, Virginia. Although he was well-known among the residents of the town and the Institute, no one could have foreseen the eventual fame and admiration he would obtain by the end of the Civil War.

The general public received its first glimpse of Jackson from newspaper stories relating details of the Rebel victory at the battle of First Manassas. In a story first printed in the *Charleston Mercury* on July 25, 1861, and later reprinted in Richmond newspapers, Confederate Brig. Gen. Barnard E. Bee, in an attempt to rally his own men, was quoted as uttering the famous words: "There is Jackson standing like a stone wall! Let us determine to die here and we will conquer! Follow me!" Although some have questioned the authenticity of the quote and whether Bee intended it as a compliment to Jackson's fortitude or as a rebuke to his immobility, the metaphor became an immediate sensation within the army and the Southern populace. From that moment, he forever became "Stonewall" Jackson and his men the "Stonewall Brigade."

Reports of Jackson's skillful maneuvering and string of victories during his subsequent Shenandoah Valley campaign of 1862 would further establish his reputation as the "Confederate hero par excellence," according to diarist Mary Chestnut. At the time, the Confederacy was badly in need of a hero: after winning the first major engagement at Manassas, the war was not going well for the South. In the western theater, New Orleans had fallen to the North and Union forces had won the hard-fought battle of Shiloh. In the east, an immense Federal army was encamped within miles of the Confederate capital at Richmond. The arrival of Jackson's army from the Shenandoah Valley coupled with Robert E. Lee's successful defense of Richmond during the Seven Days' battles helped fuel the growing sentiment among the population that the name Stonewall Jackson was synonymous with victory.[1]

A synergistic effect also developed between Jackson's battlefield successes and his religious piety. Following the May 1862 battle of McDowell during his Shenandoah Valley campaign, Jackson sent a simple telegraph to Richmond: "God blessed our arms with victory at McDowell yesterday." When the dispatch was publicized, the Southern people became ecstatic over their new-found Christian soldier. The *Daily Dispatch* (Richmond, VA) of May 29, 1862, declared Jackson "beyond all question, the hero of the war."

Analogies were frequently made between Jackson and Oliver Cromwell, the deeply religious and successful military leader of the "Roundheads" during the English Civil War of the 1600s. Cromwell's image was undergoing its own revival during the Victorian age. The Englishman had believed, much as Jackson did, that God shaped military events and handed him victories in order to carry out a predetermined mission. Sandie Pendleton, Jackson's chief of staff, wrote to his mother on October 8, 1862: "I have been reading Carlyle's 'Cromwell.' General Jackson is the exact counterpart of Oliver in every respect, as Carlyle draws him."[2]

Interest in Stonewall Jackson and comparison of him to Cromwell were not confined to the southern half of the country. Francis Lawley, Civil War correspondent for the *London Times*, wrote of Jackson in 1862: "The interest

---

1   C. Vann Woodward, ed., *Mary Chestnut's Civil War* (New Haven, CT, 1981), 428.

2   *OR* 12, pt. 1, 470; Peter Gaunt, *Oliver Cromwell* (London, 2004), 8-19; W. G. Bean, *Stonewall's Man: Sandie Pendleton* (Chapel Hill, NC, 1959), 81.

excited by this strange man is as curious as it is unprecedented." Such was the demand for photographs of "the hero of the moment" that "tens of thousands could be sold in the cities of the North." Lawley concluded his description of Jackson by commenting that some "say that once again Cromwell is walking the earth and leading his trusting and enraptured hosts to assured victory."[3]

Robert L. Dabney, former assistant adjutant general to Jackson and one of his early biographers, argued against such comparisons to Cromwell. In his 1866 book *Life and Campaigns of Lieut-Gen General Thomas J. Jackson*, Dabney wrote: "To liken Jackson to Cromwell is far more incorrect. With all the genius, both military and civic, and all the iron will of the Lord Protector, he (Jackson) had a moral and spiritual character so much more noble that they cannot be named together." Dabney believed "Cromwell's religion was essentially fanatical," while Jackson's personality was "antagonistic to fanaticism and radicalism"—a perspective many people, then and now, would consider arguable.[4]

During the battle of Antietam in September 1862, Baltimore native and *New York Tribune* reporter John Williamson Palmer anonymously composed the poem "Stonewall Jackson's Way" as a tribute to the general's character and his success in the war. References to Jackson's well-known piety were contained in the verse:

Silence! ground arms! kneel all! caps off!
Old Blue Light's going to pray;
Strangle the fool that dares to scoff!
Attention! It's his way!
Appealing from his native sod
In forma pauperis to God –
"Lay bare Thine arm; stretch forth Thy rod,
Amen!" That's "Stonewall Jackson's way."

The following year, Charles Young used verses from the poem as lyrics for his musical arrangement "Stonewall Jackson's Grand March," which became a popular patriotic song throughout the Confederate states.

---

3 *London Times*, September 20, 1862.

4 Dabney, *Life and Campaigns*, 112-115.

Sheet music to "Stonewall Jackson's Grand March" by Charles Young.
Author's Collection

Stonewall Jackson's death in May 1863 was considered a serious blow to the Confederate war effort by individuals in both the North and South. "This event is a serious and an irreparable loss to the rebel army," read an editorial in the *New York Herald* on May 14, 1863, "for it is agreed on all hands that Jackson was the most brilliant rebel general developed by this war." Raleigh E. Colston, one of Jackson's divisional commanders, believed "the star of our fortunes set when he fell." Some even wondered whether Jackson's death was some form of divine retribution for their hero worship. "How fearful the loss for the Confederacy," wrote Margaret Junkin Preston, Jackson's sister-in-law from his first marriage. "The people made an idol of him, and God has rebuked them."[5]

Among residents of the South, Jackson's death at the height of Confederate military success made him the first great martyr in the struggle for southern independence, and his stardom would reach almost mythical proportions. "Seldom in history has one been able, in so short a time, to write his name so deeply upon the hearts of his countrymen, and to raise the admiration of the world at large," stated the General Assembly of the Presbyterian Church of Columbia, South Carolina, while memorializing his death in 1863. Although Robert E. Lee had by this time also reached prominence as a central figure in the Confederacy, many in the south felt as diarist Emma LeConte did when she wrote: "He was my hero. I then admired Lee as grand, magnificent, but Jackson came nearer my heart.... Since then Lee has had the hero-worship, all—both his and Jackson's—though the dead hero will always be shrined in every Southern heart."[6]

Authors were quick to seize upon Jackson's unprecedented popularity by producing several books and biographies about him within months of his death. Surprisingly, two of the earliest works were printed in England and New York, respectively, and were not of Southern origin. Although the content of these books was largely based on newspaper clippings about Jackson and the battles in which he participated, the fact they were produced so quickly outside of the Confederacy illustrates the widespread demand the public had for information about the elusive Southern general.

Markinfield Addey expressed the sentiment of those living above the Mason-Dixon Line in the preface of his book *The Life and Military Career of Thomas Jonathan Jackson* when he wrote: "The people of the North cannot but honor the noble qualities which existed in one they had so much

---

5 R. E. Colston, "Address of Gen. R. E. Colston," *SHSP* (1893), vol. 21, 46; Elizabeth P. Allan, *The Life and Letters of Margaret Junkin Preston* (Boston and New York, 1903), 165.

6 Paper Adopted by the General Assembly of the Presbyterian Church in Session at Columbia, S. C., May, 1863, *SHSP* (August 1920), vol. 43, 103; Earl S. Miers, ed., *When the World Ended: The Diary of Emma LeConte* (New York, NY, 1957), 96.

Lithograph depicting Barbara Frietchie's confrontation with Jackson's army.
Library of Congress

cause to fear, and at whose hands they so much suffered. Whilst they must ever regret that Jackson, at the period of his doubtings, at the commencement of the Rebellion, should have finally decided to espouse the cause of the South, they cannot decline to pay fitting homage to the memory of one who was so noble in heart and so chivalric in action."[7]

Northern poets also continued to compose works about Stonewall Jackson following his death. Herman Melville, author of the novel *Moby-Dick*, wrote two poems about Jackson, while Massachusetts-born and staunch abolitionist John Greenleaf Whittier composed the popular piece *Barbara Frietchie*, which became one of the most famous Civil War poems in history. First appearing in the *Atlantic Monthly* in October 1863, Whittier's poem—rather loosely based on actual events—depicts a confrontation between Stonewall Jackson and an elderly Unionist woman

---

7 Catherine C. Hopley, *"Stonewall" Jackson, Late General of the Confederate Army* (London, 1863); Markinfield Addey, *The Life and Military Career of Thomas Jonathan Jackson* (New York, NY, 1863), 7-8.

during the Maryland campaign of 1862. In the poem, Barbara Frietchie defiantly waves a Union flag from the attic window of her house as Jackson's army marches past, proclaiming: "'Shoot, if you must, this old gray head/But spare your country's flag,' she said." Moved by her loyalty and courage, Jackson responds to his men: "'Who touches a hair of yon gray head/Dies like a dog! March on!' he said." Greenleaf concludes the poem with a tribute to both individuals:

> Barbara Frietchie's work is o'er,
> And the Rebel rides on his raids no more.
> Honor to her! and let a tear
> Fall, for her sake, on Stonewall's bier.

The greatest influence on Jackson's public persona would come from the biographies written by individuals who had direct interaction with him during the war. As each author tended to highlight a different aspect of his character, an overall—and sometimes contrasting—picture of his life developed. John Esten Cooke's first biography of Jackson, published under the pseudonym A Virginian and hastily written from May to September 1863, documented many of the colorful "eccentricities and odd ways" of Jackson that have defined his character through history. Cooke's second book, *Stonewall Jackson: A Military Biography*, published in 1866, concentrated more on Jackson's military campaigns and less on his personal life.[8]

The first authorized biography of Stonewall Jackson was Dabney's *Life and Campaigns of Lieut-Gen General Thomas J. Jackson* in 1866. Following her husband's death in 1863, Anna Jackson commissioned the Presbyterian minister to write the biography, and Dabney conducted extensive research from documents, personal interviews, and correspondence to complete the task. Dabney's theological background, however, led him to emphasize the general's spiritual nature, and he further promoted the concept of Jackson's martyrdom by writing: "He was to his

---

8 John Esten Cooke (writing as "A Virginian"), *The Life of Stonewall Jackson from Official Papers, Contemporary Narratives, and Personal Acquaintance* (New York, NY, 1863), 19.

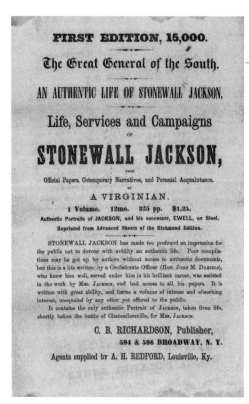

Broadside advertising John Esten Cooke's first biography of Jackson.
National Archives

fellow-citizens the man of destiny, the anointed of God to bring deliverance for his oppressed Church and Country." Despite its deeply religious overtones, Dabney's book was considered the authoritative work on Jackson's life for years following its publication.[9]

Although Anna Jackson was generally satisfied with Dabney's *Life and Campaigns*, she became increasingly displeased with the intensifying postwar image of her husband as a Cromwell-like religious fanatic. In an attempt to soften some of the harsher qualities of his character, Anna published her own book in 1892 entitled the *Life and Letters of General Thomas J. Jackson*, which was reprinted in slightly altered form in 1895 as *Memoirs of Stonewall Jackson by his Widow Mary Anna Jackson*.

Relying heavily at times on the writings of others, including Dabney and Hunter Holmes McGuire, Anna's book highlighted Jackson's domestic life, portraying him as a loving husband and father more than a brutal warrior: "He who saw only the stern, self-denying soldier in his quarters, amidst the details of the commander's duties, or on the field of battle, could scarcely comprehend the gentle sweetness of his home life." The extensive use of her

9 Wallace Hettle, "The Minister, the Martyr, and the Maxim: Robert Lewis Dabney and Stonewall Jackson Biography," *Civil War History* (2003), vol. 49; Dabney, *Life and Campaigns*, 727.

husband's surviving letters gave credence to her perspective and succeeded in presenting yet another aspect of Jackson's complex personality.[10]

Subsequent biographies of Jackson, including G. F. R. Henderson's *Stonewall Jackson and the American Civil War* in 1898 and Allen Tate's 1928 work *Stonewall Jackson: The Good Soldier*, along with numerous stories written about him in the postwar publications of the *Southern Historical Society Papers* and the *Confederate Veteran Magazine*, further enriched Jackson's actual and perceived persona. Most have contributed to the enduring Lost Cause image of Jackson as an eccentric, deeply religious military genius whose death at Chancellorsville was a significant factor leading to the eventual demise of the Confederacy.

As the real and imaginary stories regarding Stonewall Jackson continued to be told long after the war, his stature as "the idol of the people" only grew larger and larger. He became such an iconic figure, especially in the South, that his name and likeness was used to sell everything from alcohol and tobacco (whereas Jackson was neither a drinker nor a smoker) to razor blades, soap, Coca-Cola, and, ironically, life insurance. His name has also adorned numerous restaurants, hotels, public schools, and parks throughout the southern United States.[11]

In the final 22 months of his life, Thomas J. Jackson experienced a meteoric rise from obscurity to national celebrity in both the North and the South. "Few or none of those who inhabit with him the temple of Fame," Dabney wrote, "won their way to it by a career so short." In the 150 years since his death, Jackson's image has been molded and shaped through the writings of family, friends, acquaintances, and strangers. Few individuals from the American Civil War have generated as much curiosity as Stonewall Jackson, and it is likely he will remain the subject of many books and discussions for years to come.[12]

10 Jackson, *Life and Letters*, 105-106.

11 P. W. Alexander, "Confederate Chieftains," *Southern Literacy Messenger* (January 1863), vol. 35, 37.

12 Dabney, *Life and Campaigns*, 734.

Appendix III

An Interview with Author Mathew Lively

Q: *Why did you decide to write this particular book?*

A: Stonewall Jackson's death was appealing to me for multiple reasons. First, I am a West Virginia native, as was Jackson, although it was still a part of Virginia when he was born. Nonetheless, our state still considers him a native of our land. Second, I have had a long interest in Civil War history that dates back to my childhood. And last, as I became a physician, I became interested in medical history, particularly 19th century medical history. Researching Jackson's death allowed me to concentrate all my interests into one subject.

Q: *What specifically interested you initially about researching Stonewall Jackson's history?*

A: Stonewall Jackson is a well-recognized name in the state of West Virginia. His boyhood home, Jackson's Mill, is a popular state 4-H camp. There is a statue of him on the state capitol grounds, and a recreational lake and resort are named after him. Growing up in West Virginia, I became interested in Civil War history at a young age and it was a natural progression to become interested in Jackson since he is such a popular figure in my state. Then, while in medical school, I became interested in the medical aspects of the Civil War and as a natural extension, was intrigued by the medical facets of Jackson's life and death.

Q: *How did you conduct your research?*

A: Like most historical research, much of it was spent in various libraries and historical societies searching through primary sources. Fortunately, the bulk of the information was in the Virginia and Washington D.C. area, so I did not have to travel great distances. However, I have also been amazed at the amount of information that is now accessible over the Internet. More libraries are now digitalizing their holdings, so it has become much easier to obtain information electronically without ever having to leave home.

Q: *How long did it take you to research and then write the book?*

A: My guess would be about ten years in total. It started out as a desire to find out more about Jackson's death by collecting information. Soon, I discovered that no one had written a definitive account on the circumstances surrounding his death, which inspired me to try and accomplish the task. As I am not an author by trade, I worked on the project intermittently when I could find time in my otherwise busy schedule.

Q: *What makes your book unique from other things that have been written on the same topic?*

A: My book is the first full-length examination of the details surrounding the event. Most books that discuss Jackson's death do so as the last chapter in a biography of his entire life, or a short section in a Chancellorsville campaign or battle study. This book is the result of a careful analysis of the available primary source material as it relates only to the circumstances of his wounding and death. I hope that by narrowing the focus, readers will have a better understanding of what actually happened from May 2-10, 1863.

Q: *What are some features of your book that you think readers will really enjoy?*

A: I think having the story written in a narrative style makes it more pleasing to read, particularly for those who are interested in learning the story more than reading a detailed analysis of the battle or the controversies surrounding the event. But for those who want a more scholarly examination of the facts, there is an appendix that goes into that level of depth.

Q: *You mentioned there are some controversies surrounding the event. Can you elaborate on some of those?*

A: Sure. A controversy that has resurfaced recently is which road Stonewall Jackson and his staff reconnoitered down before his wounding. Many current interpretations maintain they rode down and back on the Mountain Road, as opposed to the main Plank Road. . . .

Q: *What did you mean by resurfaced? This is a long-standing controversy?*

A: Yes. This version was first proposed in the 1890s, but was quickly discounted by most of the participants directly involved in the event. I cover this in some depth, and I think readers will find the discussion of interest.

Q: *Can you share other controversies?*

A: Sure. A recent one is the medical condition that actually resulted in Jackson's death. Although the physicians involved in his care all agreed he died of pneumonia, several modern physicians have offered alternate diagnoses. Yet another controversy that has swirled since the event was whether Jackson actually said his famous last words: "Let us cross over the river and rest under the shade of the trees." All of these questions and more are discussed in Appendix I.

Q: *Were you surprised by anything you found while writing the book?*

A: I was surprised to discover that Hunter Holmes McGuire, Jackson's chief physician and friend, stepped out of the room before the general died. McGuire's account of Jackson's final moments are the most cited source for documentation of his last words, and yet McGuire admits in an early letter to Jed Hotchkiss that he wasn't actually in the room at the time and never heard Jackson say the words.

Q: *What do you think of the medical care Jackson received at the time?*

A: It was the standard of care for the time. It's easy to look back and criticize what we realize today were misguided and even harmful treatments, but the 1860s were still at the end of the medical "Dark Ages" in the sense of scientific knowledge. The germ theory had yet to be advanced, so the physicians of the time did not have a grasp of how diseases were transmitted, and consequently did not have an appreciation of the need for sterile technique. Because the germ theory did not exist, neither did antibiotics exist to kill the disease-causing bacteria. Since the physicians had a basic misunderstanding of the science behind disease, they also had a misunderstanding of how to treat disease. There were, however, some success stories at the time. For example, morphine was used successfully to treat pain, quinine was used to treat malaria, and anesthetic was used to perform surgery. Some of Jackson's care was no doubt detrimental to his condition, but the physicians did the best they could with what they knew at the time. I'm sure a hundred years from now future physicians will look back on what we do today and think some of it as being archaic.

Q: *What was the most difficult aspect of writing this book?*

A: Sorting through the various first person accounts of the event and determining which ones appeared to be the most accurate representation of the facts. This was made more difficult because some of the details in the accounts were contradictory, even when written by the same person many years apart. Interpreting history is not an exact science and making decisions on which details to accept and which to reject is not an easy task when the event happened 150 years ago.

Q: *Did you come away with any new perspectives or opinions of Stonewall Jackson?*

A: I always knew Jackson was a religious individual, but until writing the book, I did not have an appreciation for the depth of his religious convictions. His faith seemed to pervade every fiber of his being. Although he seemed to approach devotion to God as his personal duty, his duty as a soldier seemed to take precedence over his deeply religious convictions once the fighting began. He could turn from being a pious, merciful human being one second to being a brutal, merciless soldier the next. His personality was a remarkable litany of contrasts.

Q: *Why do you think the events in your book are so misunderstood?*

A: I think, in part, because in the 150 years since the event, there have been some contradictory accounts published in various books and magazines. Jackson didn't survive the ordeal, so we have had to rely on others to provide the details and some of those individuals may have embellished the facts and their involvement in the event for their own benefit. Also, many interpretations and retellings of the event have relied on only one or two accounts, which in turn, can lead to a misunderstanding of what actually occurred.

Q: *Thank you for your time, we appreciate it.*

A: You're welcome.

Bibliography

Primary Sources

Manuscript Collections and Letters

Carson, John J. Letter to Mary C. Higgs, January 20, 1916. Copy is in author's
    possession
Denver (CO) Medical Library
Florida Atlantic University (FAU)
Fredericksburg and Spotsylvania National Military Park (FSNMP)
Harvard University
    A. C. Hamlin Collection (ACHC)
Library of Congress (LC)
    Abraham Lincoln Papers, Series 1, General Correspondence, 1833-1916
    Hotchkiss Papers
    Jubal Anderson Early Papers
Library of Virginia (LVA)
    Dabney-Jackson Collection
Museum of the Confederacy (MOC)
    Thomas J. Jackson Collection
New York Historical Society (NYHS)
    Miscellaneous Manuscripts

University of North Carolina, Southern Historical Collection (SHC)
    Charles William Dabney Papers
University of South Carolina
    Crawford Family Papers
University of Virginia (UVA)
    Special Collections
Virginia Historical Society (VHS)
    Charles J. Faulkner Papers
    Jed Hotchkiss Papers
    Lee Family Papers
Virginia Military Institute (VMI) Archives and Museum
    Sandie Pendleton Papers
West Virginia University
    Roy Bird Cook Collection

Periodicals

CV = *Confederate Veteran Magazine*
SHSP = *Southern Historical Society Papers*

Colston, R. E. "Address Before the Ladies Memorial Association." *SHSP* 21 (1893): 38-49.

Craige, John H. "The Wilderness Maneuvers." *Marine Corps Gazette* 6, no. 4 (1921): 418-423.

Early, Jubal A. "Stonewall Jackson—The Story of His Being an Astrologer Refuted—An Eyewitness Describes How He Was Wounded." *SHSP* 6 (1878): 261-282.

"Field Notes at Chancellorsville from Stuart and Jackson." *SHSP* 11(1883): 137-138.

Hairston, Peter W. "The Civil War Diary of Peter W. Hairston, Volunteer Aide to Major General Jubal A. Early, November 7–December 4, 1863." Ed. Everard H. Smith. *North Carolina Historical Review* 67, no. 1 (1990): 59-86.

Jones, J. William. "Stonewall Jackson: Personal Reminiscences and Anecdotes of his Character—Recollections of Him by Dr. J. William Jones, Formerly Chaplain of the Army of Northern Virginia." *SHSP* 19 (1891): 145-164.

Kinsolving, Roberta Corbin. "Memories of Moss Neck in the Winter of 1862-63." *CV* 20 (January 1912): 24-26.

Kyle, David. "Jackson's Guide When Shot." *CV* 4 (September 1896): 308- 309.

Lee, Fitzhugh. "Chancellorsville – Address of General Fitzhugh Lee before the Virginia Division, A. N. V. Association, October 29th, 1879." *SHSP* 7 (1879): 545-585.

McGuire, Hunter Holmes. "Career and Character of General T. J. Jackson." *SHSP* 25 (1897): 91-112.

———. "Death of Stonewall Jackson." *SHSP* 14 (1886): 154-162.

———. "How Stonewall Jackson Died." *De Bow's Review* 8 (1870): 477- 478.

———. "Last Wound of the Late Gen. Jackson (Stonewall)—The Amputation of the Arm—His Last Moments and Death." *Richmond Medical Journal* 1 (1866): 403-412.

———. "Reminiscences of the Famous Leader by Dr. Hunter McGuire, Chief Surgeon of the Second Corps of the Army of Northern Virginia." *SHSP* 19 (1891): 298-323.

Moorman, Marcellus N. "Narrative of Events and Observations Connected with the Wounding of General T. J. (Stonewall) Jackson." *SHSP* 30 (1902): 110-117.

Morrison, Joseph G. "Stonewall Jackson at Chancellorsville." *CV* 8 (May 1905): 229-232.

[———]. "Wounding of Lieutenant-General T. J. Jackson." *The Land We Love* 1 (July 1866): 179-182.

"Oil-Cloth Coat in which Jackson Received His Mortal Wound." *SHSP* 19 (1891): 324-326.

Palmer, William H. "Another Account of It." *CV* 8 (May 1905): 232-233.

"Paper Adopted by the General Assembly of the Presbyterian Church in Session at Columbia, SC, May 1863." *SHSP* 43 (1920): 103-105.

Potter, H. L. *The National Tribune*, October 18, 1888.

Randolph, William F. "General Jackson's Mortal Wound." *SHSP* 29 (1901): 329-337.

Rennolds, Albert. "Virginia Reminiscences." *CV* 5 (February 1897): 50-53.

Sanders, Christopher C. "Battle of Chancellorsville." *SHSP* 29 (1901): 166-172.

"Stonewall Jackson's Death." *SHSP* 10 (1882): 143.

Talcott, Thomas Mann Randolph. "General Lee's Strategy at the Battle of Chancellorsville." *SHSP* 34 (1906): 1-27.

Taylor, Murray F. "Stonewall Jackson's Death." *CV* 7 (October 1904): 492-494.

Thompson, J. S. *The National Tribune*, February 14, 1889.

"Unveiling of the Statue of General Ambrose Powell Hill at Richmond, Virginia, May 30, 1892." *SHSP* 20 (1892): 352-392.

Books

B&L = Battles and Leaders of the Civil War
OR = The War of the Rebellion: A Compilation of the Official Records . . .

Alexander, Edward P. *Fighting for the Confederacy: The Personal Recollections of General Edward Porter Alexander.* Ed. Gary W. Gallagher. Chapel Hill: University of North Carolina Press, 1989.

Bates, Samuel P. "Hooker's Comments on Chancellorsville." *B&L*, vol. 3, pt. 1, 215-223.

Douglas, Henry Kyd. *I Rode with Stonewall*. Chapel Hill: University of North Carolina Press, 1940.

Eggleston, George C. *A Captain in the Ranks: A Romance of Affairs*. New York: A. S. Barnes & Co., 1904.

Goode, James E. *The Life of Thomas J. Jackson by a Cadet*. 2nd ed. Richmond: Author, 1864.

Hotchkiss, Jedediah. *Make Me a Map of the Valley: The Civil War Journal of Stonewall Jackson's Topographer*. Ed. Archie P. McDonald. Dallas: Southern Methodist University Press, 1973.

——. and William Allan. *Chancellorsville: Embracing the Operations of the Army of Northern Virginia from the First Battle of Fredericksburg to the Death of Lieutenant-General Jackson*. New York: D. Van Nostrand, 1867.

Houck, Peter W. *Confederate Surgeon: The Personal Recollections of E. A. Craighill*. Lynchburg, VA: H. E. Howard, 1989.

Howard, Oliver O. "The Eleventh Corps at Chancellorsville." *B&L*, vol. 3, pt. 1, 189-202.

Huey, Pennock, and Andrew Wells. "The Charge of the Eighth Pennsylvania Cavalry." *B&L*, vol. 3, pt. 1, 186-188.

Imboden, John D. "Incidents of the First Bull Run." *B&L*, vol. 1. pt. 1, 229-239.

——. "Stonewall Jackson in the Shenandoah." *B&L*, vol. 2, pt. 1, 282-298.

Jackson, Mary Anna. *Life and Letters of General Thomas J. Jackson*. New York: Harper & Brothers, 1892.

——. *Memoirs of Stonewall Jackson by his Widow Mary Anna Jackson*. Louisville, KY: Prentice Press, 1895.

Johnson, Robert Underwood, and Clarence Clough Buel, eds. *Battles and Leaders of the Civil War: Being for the Most Part Contributions by Union and Confederate Officers*. 4 vols. New York: Century Company, 1887-1888.

Jones, J. William. *Christ in Camp or Religion in Lee's Army*. Richmond: B. F. Johnson & Co., 1887.

Jones, John B. *A Rebel War Clerk's Diary*. 2 vols. Philadelphia: J. B. Lippincott & Co., 1866.

Lincoln, Abraham. *Collected Works of Abraham Lincoln*. 9 vols. Ed. Roy P. Basler. New Brunswick, NJ: Rutgers University Press, 1953.

Long, Armistead L. *Memoirs of Robert E. Lee*. Secaucus, NJ: Blue and Grey Press, 1983.

Longstreet, James. "The Battle of Fredericksburg." *B&L*, vol. 3, pt. 1, 70-85.

McGuire, Hunter H., and George L. Christian. *The Confederate Cause and Conduct in the War Between The States*. Richmond, VA: L. H. Jenkins, 1907.

McLaughlin, William. *Ceremonies Connected with the Unveiling of the Bronze Statue of Gen. Thomas J. (Stonewall) Jackson at Lexington, Virginia, July 21, 1891*. Baltimore: John Murphy & Co., 1891.

McLaurin, William H. "Eighteenth Regiment." *Histories of the Several Regiments and Battalions from North Carolina in the Great War 1861-65*. Ed. Walter Clark. Goldsboro, NC: Nash Brothers Book and Job Printers, 1901.

Malles, Ed, ed. *Bridge Building in Wartime: Colonel Wesley Brainerd's Memoir of the 50th New York Volunteer Engineers*. Knoxville: University of Tennessee Press, 1997.

Maury, Dabney H. *Recollections of a Virginian in the Mexican, Indian, and Civil Wars*. New York: Charles Scribner's Sons, 1894.

Revere, Joseph W. *Keel and Saddle, a Retrospect of Forty Years of Military and Naval Service*. Boston: Osgood and Company, 1872.

Seymour, William J. *The Civil War Memoirs of Captain William J. Seymour. Reminiscences of a Louisiana Tiger*. Ed. Terry L. Jones. Baton Rouge, LA: Louisiana State University Press, 1991.

Smith, James Power. "Stonewall Jackson and Chancellorsville. A Paper Read Before the Military Historical Society of Massachusetts, on the First of March, 1904." Richmond: Confederate Veterans, 1904.

——. "Stonewall Jackson's Last Battle." *B&L*. Vol. 3, pt. 1, 203-214.

Sutton, Thomas H. "Additional Sketch. Eighteenth Regiment." *Histories of the Several Regiments and Battalions from North Carolina in the Great War 1861-65*. Ed. Walter Clark. Goldsboro, NC: Nash Brothers Book and Job Printers, 1901.

Taylor, Richard. *Destruction and Reconstruction: Personal Experiences of the Late War*. New York: D. Appleton and Company, 1879.

The War of the Rebellion: A Compilation of the Official Records of the Union and Confederate Armies. Series 1, vol. 25, pt. 1. Washington: Government Printing Office, 1889.

——. Series 1, vol. 25, pt. 2. Washington: Government Printing Office, 1889.

——. Series 2, vol. 4. Washington: Government Printing Office, 1899.

Whitaker, Spier. "The Wounding of Jackson." *Histories of the Several Regiments and Battalions from North Carolina in the Great War 1861–65*. Ed. Walter Clark. Goldsboro, NC: Nash Brothers Book and Job Printers, 1901.

Newspapers

The Daily Constitution (Atlanta, GA)
Boston Daily Globe
Charleston (SC) Mercury
The Free-Lance (Fredericksburg, VA)

Herald-Progress (Ashland, VA)
Lexington (VA) Gazette
London Times
National Tribune
New York Herald
New York Times
Daily Dispatch (Richmond, VA)
Richmond (VA) Enquirer
The Sentinel (Richmond, VA)
Daily Richmond Whig
Daily Morning Chronicle (Washington, D.C.)

Secondary Sources

Periodicals

Alexander, P. W. "Confederate Chieftains." *Southern Literacy Messenger* 35, no. 1 (1863): 34-38.

Bean, W. G. "Stonewall Jackson's Jolly Chaplain, Beverly Tucker Lacy." *West Virginia History* 29 (1968): 77-96.

Faust, Drew G. "Numbers on Top of Numbers: Counting the Civil War Dead." *Journal of Military History* 70, no. 4 (2006): 995-1,009.

Gorham, L. Whittington. "What Was the Cause of Stonewall Jackson's Death?" *Archives of Internal Medicine* 111 (1963): 540-544.

Hacker, J. David. "A Census-based Count of Civil War Dead." *Civil War History* 57, no. 4 (2011): 307-348.

Haines, Joe D. "What Killed Stonewall Jackson." *Journal of the Oklahoma State Medical Association* 91, no. 4 (1998): 162-165.

Happel, Ralph. "The Chancellors of Chancellorsville." *The Virginia Magazine of History and Biography* 71, no. 3 (1963): 259-277.

Hettle, Wallace. "The Minister, the Martyr, and the Maxim: Robert Lewis Dabney and Stonewall Jackson Biography." *Civil War History* 49, no. 4 (2003): 353-369.

Koch, Timothy R., and Joseph B. Kirsner. "Chronic Gastrointestinal Symptoms of Thomas 'Stonewall' Jackson following Mexican-American War Exposure: A Medical Hypothesis." *Military Medicine* 172, no. 1 (2007): 6-8.

Lewis, Samuel E. "General T. J. Jackson (Stonewall) and his Medical Director, Hunter McGuire, M.D., at Winchester, May 1862." *The Southern Practitioner* 24, no. 10 (1902): 553-564.

Lively, Mathew W. "Early Onset Pneumonia Following Pulmonary Contusion: The Case of Stonewall Jackson." *Military Medicine* 177, no. 3 (2012): 315-317.

———. "Stonewall Jackson and the Old Man's Friend." *Journal of Medical Biography* 19 (2011): 84-88.

Riggs, David F. "Stonewall Jackson's Raincoat." *Civil War Times Illustrated* 16 (July 1977): 37-41.

Rozear, Marvin P., and Joseph C. Greenfield. "'Let Us Cross Over the River': The Final Illness of Stonewall Jackson." *Virginia Magazine of History and Biography* 103, no. 1 (1995): 29-46.

Sanders, Tom E. "He is Dead, Yet He Liveth." *Civil War Times* 46 (January 2008): 38-39.

Smith, Alan D. "Stonewall Jackson and His Surgeon, Hunter McGuire." *Bulletin of the N.Y. Academy of Medicine* 49 (1973): 594-609.

Smith, Beverly C. "The Last Illness and Death of General Thomas Jonathan (Stonewall) Jackson." *Virginia Military Institute Alumni Review* 51 (1975): 8-13.

"Stonewall Jackson and the Henderson Hydropath." *Samaritan Health Newsletter*, no. 42 (September 2008): 1-4.

Books

Addey, Markinfield. *The Life and Military Career of Thomas Jonathan Jackson.* New York: Charles T. Evans, 1863.

Allan, Elizabeth Preston. *The Life and Letters of Margaret Junkin Preston.* Boston and New York: Houghton, Mifflin and Company, 1903.

Atkinson, William B. *A Biographical Dictionary of Contemporary Physicians and Surgeons.* 2nd ed. Philadelphia: D. G. Brinton, 1880.

Bean, W. G. *Stonewall's Man: Sandie Pendleton.* Chapel Hill: University of North Carolina Press, 1959.

Bigelow, John. *Chancellorsville.* New York: Smithmark Publishers, 1995.

Bruce, Philip A., ed. *History of Virginia.* 6 vols. Chicago: American Historical Society, 1924.

Chambers, Lenoir. *Stonewall Jackson.* 2 vols. New York: William Morrow & Co., 1959.

Chisolm, J. Julian. *A Manual of Military Surgery for the Use of Surgeons in the Confederate States Army with Explanatory Plates of all Useful Operations.* Columbia, SC: Evans and Cogswell, 1864.

Clark, Walter, ed. *Histories of the Several Regiments and Battalions from North Carolina in the Great War 1861-65.* 5 vols. Raleigh, NC: E. M. Uzzell, 1901.

Cooke, John Esten. *The Life of Stonewall Jackson from Official Papers, Contemporary Narratives, and Personal Acquaintance.* New York: Charles B. Richardson, 1863.

——. *Stonewall Jackson: A Military Biography*. New York: D. Appleton and Company, 1866.

Dabney, Robert L. *Life and Campaigns of Lieut-Gen. Thomas J. Jackson*. New York: Blelock & Co., 1866.

Finkbeiner, Walter E., Philip C. Ursell, and Richard L. Davis. *Autopsy Pathology: A Manual and Atlas*. 2nd ed. Philadelphia: Saunders, 2009.

Fourth Annual Report of the Library Board of the Virginia State Library 1906-1907. Richmond: Public Printing, 1907.

Freeman, Douglas Southall. *Lee's Lieutenants*. 3 vols. New York: Charles Scribner's Sons, 1942.

——. *R. E. Lee: A Biography*. New York: Charles Scribner's Sons, 1934.

Gaunt, Peter. *Oliver Cromwell*. London: The British Library, 2004.

Hamlin, Augustus C. *The Battle of Chancellorsville: The Attack of Stonewall Jackson and his Army Upon the Right Flank of the Army of the Potomac at Chancellorsville, Virginia, on Saturday Afternoon, May 2, 1863*. Bangor, ME: Augustus Hamlin, 1896.

Harrison, Noel G. *Chancellorsville Battlefield Sites*. Lynchburg, VA: H. E. Howard, 1990.

Henderson, George Francis Robert. *Stonewall Jackson and the American Civil War*. London: Longmans, Green, and Co., 1913.

Hettle, Wallace. *Inventing Stonewall Jackson*. Baton Rouge, LA: Louisiana State University Press, 2011.

Hopley, Catherine C. *"Stonewall" Jackson, Late General of the Confederate Army*. London: Chapman and Hall, 1863.

Hueske, Edward E. *Practical Analysis and Reconstruction of Shooting Incidents*. Boca Raton, FL: CRC Press, 2006.

Keen, William W. *Addresses and Other Papers*. Philadelphia: W. B. Saunders & Co., 1905.

Koonce, Donald B. *Doctor to the Front: The Recollections of Confederate Surgeon Thomas Fanning Wood*. Knoxville: University of Tennessee Press, 2000.

Krick, Robert K. *The Smoothbore Volley that Doomed the Confederacy*. Baton Rouge, LA: Louisiana State University Press, 2002.

Lee, Robert E. *Recollections and Letters of Robert E. Lee*. New York: Doubleday, Page & Co., 1904.

Lee, Susan P. *Memoirs of William Nelson Pendleton*, D.D. Philadelphia: J. B. Lippincott Company, 1893.

McClellan, Henry B. *The Life and Campaigns of Major-General J. E. B. Stuart*. Boston: Houghton, Mifflin and Company, 1885.

McMullen, Glenn L. *A Surgeon with Stonewall Jackson: The Civil War Letters of Dr. Harvey Black*. Baltimore: Butternut and Blue, 1995.

Miers, Earl S., ed. *When the World Ended: The Diary of Emma LeConte*. New York: Oxford University Press, 1957.

Osler, William. *The Principles and Practice of Medicine.* 3rd ed. New York: D. Appleton and Company, 1898.

Otis, George A. *Medical and Surgical History of the War of the Rebellion.* Washington, D.C.: Government Printing Office, 1876.

Record of Events Database. *Valley of the Shadow: Two Communities in the American Civil War.* Charlottesville: Virginia Center for Digital History, University of Virginia.

Robertson, James I. *General A. P. Hill: The Story of a Confederate Warrior.* New York: Random House, 1987.

———. *Stonewall Jackson: The Man, The Soldier, The Legend.* New York: Macmillan Publishing, 1997.

Sears, Stephen W. *Chancellorsville.* Boston: Houghton Mifflin Co., 1996.

Smart, Charles. *The Medical and Surgical History of the War of the Rebellion.* Washington, D.C.: Government Printing Office, 1888.

Topographic Maps of Chancellorsville and Salem Church Battlefields, Spotsylvania County, Virginia. U.S.: Department of the Interior, Library of Congress, 1932.

Transactions of the Medical and Chirurgical Faculty of the State of Maryland and its Eighty-Fourth Annual Session. Baltimore: Press of Isaac Friedenwald, 1882.

Wise, Jennings C. *The Military History of the Virginia Military Institute from 1839 to 1865.* Lynchburg, VA: J. P. Bell Company, 1915.

Woodward, C. Vann, ed. *Mary Chestnut's Civil War.* New Haven, CT: Yale University Press, 1981.

Index

About the Author

Mathew W. Lively is a practicing physician and Professor of Internal Medicine and Pediatrics at the West Virginia University School of Medicine. The recipient of two master's degrees in addition to his medical degree, he has been an active teacher of medical students and resident physicians for the past fifteen years.

A lifelong student of both the Civil War and medical history, Dr. Lively is the author of many scientific articles published in the medical literature. *Calamity at Chancellorsville: The Wounding and Death of Confederate General Stonewall Jackson* (2013) is his first book.